NATURE IN VANCOUVER

A GUIDE TO THE BEST PLACES TO FIND BIRDS, ANIMALS, INSECTS, MARINE LIFE, PLANTS AND FLOWERS IN AND AROUND VANCOUVER

VANCOUVER NATURAL HISTORY SOCIETY

CAVENDISH BOOKS
VANCOUVER

Published in Canada by:

Cavendish Books Inc.,
Unit 5, 801 West 1st Street,
North Vancouver, B.C. V7P 1A4

Copyright 1996   The Vancouver Natural History Society

Canadian Cataloguing in Publication Data

Nature in Vancouver

  Includes bibliographical references and index
  ISBN 0-929050-59-2

        1. Natural areas - British Columbia - Vancouver - Guidebooks.
2. Natural history - British Columbia - Vancouver - Guidebooks
3. Vancouver (B.C.) - Guidebooks.   I. Vancouver Natural History Society
QH106.2B7N39 1996   508.711'33   C96-910532-0

CONTENTS

ACKNOWLEDGEMENTS

The suggestion to produce *Nature in Vancouver* as a guide book to places accessible by public transportation was made by Bill Merilees. The descriptions of the various destinations were written by:

Terry and Rosemary Taylor (Bloedel Conservatory, Camosun Bog, Southlands, Steveston); Valentin Schaefer (Downtown, Renfrew Ravine, Byrne Creek Ravine, Central Park, Robert Burnaby Park, Burns Bog); Daphne Solecki (Jericho Beach Park, Stanley Park); Jennifer Getsinger (Kitsilano Foreshore, Caulfeild Park, Kanaka Creek); Bill Merilees (Musqueam Park, Newcastle Island); Don Benson (Queen Elizabeth Park, Stanley Park (gardens), UBC Botanical Garden, VanDusen Botanical Garden); Margaret Flaherty (Burnaby Mountain); Doreen Dewell (Mundy Park); Audrey Viken (Ambleside Park, Capilano River Regional Park, Hollyburn Ridge, Lighthouse Park); Al Grass (Mt Seymour Provincial Park, Boundary Bay, Galiano Island); Rick Simpson (Port Moody Shoreline Park); Kris Bauder (Richmond Nature Park); Rex Kenner (Blackie Spit); George Clulow (Burnaby Lake and Deer Lake).

The project to produce this publication was coordinated by Bill Merilees and Val Schaefer. Editing and word processing were done by Val Schaefer. Proof reading was done by Elizabeth Griffiths, Linda Kingston, Daphne Solecki, and Christine Star. Maps were produced by Ian Parfitt and Doug Kragh. The map of Burnaby Mountain was provided by the Burnaby Mountain Preservation Society. The maps of Robert Burnaby Park and Central Park are courtesy The City of Burnaby. The map of Mundy Park is courtesy the City of Coquitlam. The cover photo of Mute Swans at Lost Lagoon in Stanley Park was taken by Maureen Rutter. Final layout and design was by Derek Hayes.

Financial support was provided in part by the Friends of the Environment Foundation, customers of Canada Trust, and by the Special Projects Fund of the Vancouver Natural History Society.

Photographs were all taken by members of the Vancouver Natural History Society. Photo credits are as follows:

Bill Merilees (p. 10, 11, 18, 20, 22, 28, 34, 38, 43, 44, 50, 53, 54, 58, 64, 72, 74, 82, 84, 86, 87, 88, 91, 104, 110, 111);
Al Grass (p. 9, 16, 26, 30, 36, 48, 57, 60, 62, 70, 73, 77, 81, 92, 98, 99, 100, 103);
Osbourne Shaw (p. 8, 37, 47, 78);
John Ireland (p. 102).

INTRODUCTION

Most of us live in cities. We generally do not think of a city as wildlife habitat, or of being part of a globally important ecosystem. Cities are generally considered to have little or no natural value. Nothing can be further from the truth. Most cities are strategically located at river mouths or at the entrance of straits and fjords. These are often rich with natural productivity and biodiversity.

Vancouver and its neighbouring municipalities occur along Georgia Strait, the Fraser River Estuary, and Burrard Inlet. This region is on the Pacific Flyway, home to millions of birds who live and breed here, or are stopping over on their way between northern Canada/Alaska and Central/South America. It is also used by millions of salmon whose fry and smolts feed along the foreshore, and where the adults themselves travel through on their way to spawn in the many tributaries of the Fraser River farther inland.

Greater Vancouver has many important environmentally sensitive areas, several of which are surviving ecosystem fragments representing some of the original habitat in the region. Some is second growth which has established itself after the initial onslaught of logging in the region about a hundred years ago. What are some of these areas? They are: Stanley Park, Pacific Spirit Regional Park, Burnaby Mountain, Burns Bog, Camosun Bog, Roberts and Sturgeon Banks, Port Moody Flats, Burnaby Lake, Deer Lake, Mundy Park, and hundreds of streams, many with ravines, just to name a few.

We also have many artificially created ecosystems which are exceptional in their beauty and biodiversity. Some include: VanDusen Botanical Gardens, Queen Elizabeth Park, the University of British Columbia Botanical Garden and Stanley Park Gardens.

Even in the heart of the city nature surrounds us in the most unexpected ways. Flocks of birds may descend on a tree in a small corner park downtown, or use a climbing vine on a wall for shelter overnight. There are stickleback trout in the smallest of ponds next to railway lines. Even a single street tree may have a small food chain on its leaves with aphids, aphid eggs, ants and ladybugs.

Nature in Vancouver is a guide to the natural wonders of Vancouver and surrounding areas, at all levels - from Stanley Park to the street corners. The suggested locations are all accessible by public transit and all present rich opportunities for discovery.

We live with nature every day. It does not only exist in far off places accessible by canoe or backpacking. Nature is here for us to enjoy wherever we are, each day.

Everyone who explores nature must understand the inherent risks and attendant responsibilities for safety and responsible conduct. Although the authors and publisher have made every effort to present accurate and up-to-date information, the reader must be aware that circumstances change and that the authors and publisher accept no responsibility for any injury, loss or damage arising from this book. Users must dress appropriately for the weather and the area, inform others of their plans and estimated return times, carry safety equipment, follow posted signs and warnings and at all times act in a safe and responsible manner.

Check bus and ferry schedules before leaving on any excursion.

	Phone	Talking Yellow Pages	
BC Transit	521-0400	299-9000	2233
West Van "Blue Buses"	985-7777	n/a	
BC Ferries	277-0277	299-9000	9558

Useful reference books on the flora and fauna of the Vancouver area are listed in the bibliography on p. 112.

The Vancouver Natural History Society can be contacted at P.O. Box 3021, Vancouver, B.C. V6B 3X5

Events and Information line and Bird Alert is (604) 737-3074

Mute Swan

BLOEDEL CONSERVATORY

The Bloedel Floral Conservatory is Vancouver's display of tropical plants. Its large geodesic dome is located in Queen Elizabeth Park, atop Little Mountain, where there is also a fine panoramic view of the North Shore mountains. About 500 species of plants are displayed. Many of these are identified — certainly enough for the casual visitor, but unfortunately not sufficient for the keen horticulturist or botanist. A pond with koi, as well as a number of tropical birds, add to the botanical attractions.

Best Time to Visit: All year.

Bus Service: The #15 Cambie (South on Cambie Street). Get off at 33rd Avenue and Cambie Street. Bus travel time is 10 minutes from Broadway and Cambie.

Access: Cross Cambie Street and walk east up 33rd Avenue, on the south side of Queen Elizabeth Park. There is a large directional sign in front of you. Go straight ahead towards the large dome of the conservatory. It is a 10 minute walk from the bus stop. See map on page 26.

The conservatory is open 7 days a week, except Christmas Day. The hours of operation vary from summer to winter, and between weekends and weekdays. Admission is currently $3.00. Please call beforehand for changes in hours and price. Telephone: 257-8570.

Wooly Caterpillar

Western Yew

CAMOSUN BOG

This small sphagnum bog is part of Pacific Spirit Regional Park. It is possibly the oldest bog in the Lower Mainland, and is the only surviving example of this type of ecosystem between Boundary Road and Point Grey. Peat-associated plants such as shore pine, Labrador tea, swamp laurel, the insectivorous sundew, cranberry, and cloudberry - which reaches its southern limit in Greater Vancouver - can still be found here. The Vancouver Natural History Society, and the GVRD have made efforts to preserve this unique site by cutting back invading hemlock trees and raising the water table over the summer.

Best Time to Visit: The bog pond is accessible via boardwalk all year. Bog flowers bloom during May. The white blooms of Labrador tea appear first, and the pink swamp laurel later.

Bus Service: The #25 UBC (West via King Edward Avenue, Dunbar Street, and 16th Avenue). Get off at 16th and Camosun. Walking time is about 3 minutes south from the bus stop.

Access: Walk south on Camosun Street to the street end, just past 19th Avenue. A bark mulch trail runs south a short distance, beneath the powerline, and then turns west, where a boardwalk allows close inspection of the bog flora near the pond.

Hazards: The boardwalk may be slippery when wet. Visitors are not allowed off the trail as this is a very fragile environment. Dogs are not allowed in Pacific Spirit Regional Park or the bog. Sixteenth Avenue has a great deal of traffic in rush hour, so use the pedestrian-operated light at the Camosun intersection to cross.

Labrador Tea

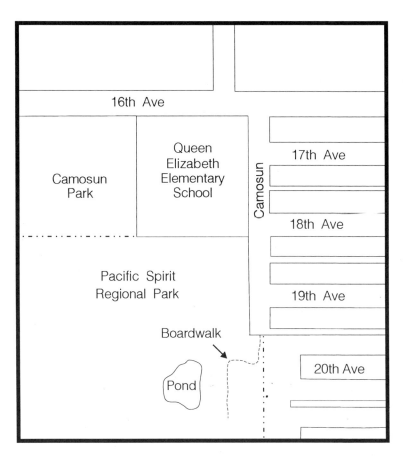

16th Ave

Camosun Park

Queen Elizabeth Elementary School

Camosun

17th Ave

18th Ave

Pacific Spirit Regional Park

19th Ave

Boardwalk

Pond

20th Ave

Location of Camosun Bog

DOWNTOWN VANCOUVER
A SELF-GUIDED FIELD TRIP

You would not expect to find evidence of nature in the financial and office districts of downtown Vancouver. However, it is there for those with an interest and a keen eye for the natural world. Of course there are no expansive natural areas (although Stanley Park is nearby), but there are native plants used in landscaping, innovative designs in fountains and courtyards, and symbolic representations of nature through art and architecture.

The plants and animals, along with their artistic representations, create an exciting presence of nature in an otherwise potentially sterile urban landscape. Not only do they provide a constant reminder that we are part of a local ecosystem and the biosphere but they are also an important example that there is more to consider than just financial gain. Nature downtown also provides a valuable opportunity for people to stay in touch with their spiritual values while surrounded by economic and business interests.

The small isolated patches of plant life and nature art hopefully will inspire the creation of similar efforts in the future. They can serve as nuclei for an even greater natural presence to grow and make our city core richer and more inviting. With a little attention and encouragement we can make the downtown greener and perhaps attract more wildlife.

This self-guided field trip highlights 16 locations in downtown Vancouver where a sense of nature is present. It includes unique landscape designs and artwork that are in keeping with the composition and spirit of our local environment. The field trip begins at the Burrard SkyTrain station and follows a figure-8 pattern around the station. It takes about one hour to see all of the sights.

"NATURE DOWNTOWN" ITINERARY

1. Burrard SkyTrain Station
    - ravine effect in landscaping, containing rhododendrons, sword ferns, and a fountain

2. National Bank Building - 555 Burrard
    - native vegetation in a fountain with horsetail and sword fern

3.   Montreal Trust Centre - 510 Burrard
- bronze sculpture of two killer whales

4.   999 W Hastings
- rhododendrons and large oak trees in terraced front of building

5.   Marine Building - 355 Burrard
- Canada Geese and marine organisms relief sculpture at entrance

6.   Foot of Burrard
- view of Burrard Inlet and Stanley Park. Look for sea birds (goldeneye, scoters, scaup, harlequin), gulls, and harbour seals

7.   Waterfront Centre Hotel - Cordova Street
- terraced ravine with grasses in landscaping

8.   200 Granville Street
- pine trees in large cement pots decorate parking lot

9.   750 W Pender
- bronze sculpture of seven Canada Geese in flight

10.   Bentall Centre
- fountains with natural waterfall effect and pine trees

11.   Hyland Building - 1190 Melville
- large mural of killer whales

12.   1200 block Melville
- terraced building with vines

13.   Wang Building - 1500 W Georgia
- 70 metre long waterfall fountain

14.   1100 block Aberni
- West Coast Rain Forest mural

15.   Robson Plaza
- Bird of Spring bronze Inuit sculpture

16.   Robson Square
- terraced fountain and extensive landscaping

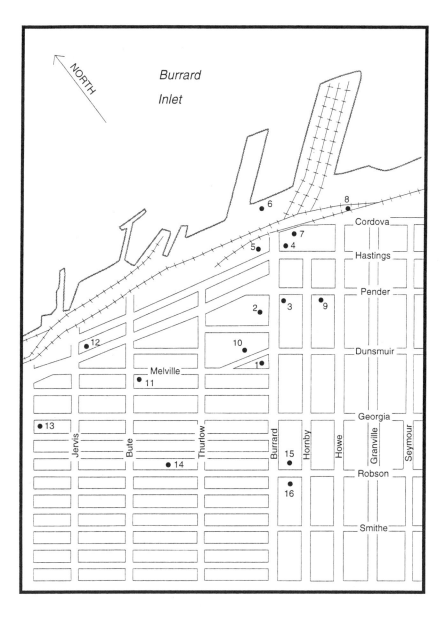

Location of downtown features referred to in text

Crab Spider

JERICHO BEACH PARK

Jericho is one of the best of our city parks for birding. Although at 54 ha (130 ac) the park is less than one sixth the area of Stanley Park, 180 species of birds (about 20 breeding) are regularly to be found there. Within its boundaries the park provides a mix of woodland, rough meadow, freshwater marsh and ponds, scrub, flat grassy areas, sandy foreshore and a saltwater bay.

Along the beach, the visitor may walk (at low tide) east along the last remaining section of natural rocky shoreline to Kits Point and Burrard Bridge or west to the Point Grey headland and the University of British Columbia campus, looking at gulls, herons and eagles feeding along the exposed sand flats. There are several concession stands, and washrooms to the west, none to the east.

Best time to Visit: *Birds* - the greatest numbers and variety are to be found during the winter months through to spring migration in mid-May. *Flowers* - although attractive during spring and early summer, most are introduced species.

Bus Service: Jericho Park is served by the #4 UBC and #42 Spanish Banks buses and is only a short walk from the #7 Dunbar stop at West 4th Avenue and Alma Street. Bus travel time is 20-30 minutes from downtown Vancouver, and 10 minutes from UBC.

Access: The park is located on the north side of West 4th Avenue and can be entered at several points between Wallace and Discovery Streets. The least busy part of the park is the area that slopes down from West 4th Avenue to the ponds. From the high ground the views across Burrard Inlet - freighters, yachts, mountains and downtown Vancouver - are spectacular. From the ponds to the beach the park becomes increasingly busy with joggers, cyclists, dogs, etc.

If you enter the park from the east boundary one main path leads to the beach, two others will take you north and south of the ponds and marshes and through some mixed deciduous woodland areas, mostly red alder, bigleaf maple and vine maple with an understorey of salmonberry and brambles. It is possible to criss-cross the park east/west by several different routes.

Hazards: In winter the trails across the upper terrain can get very wet and will soak ordinary sneakers.

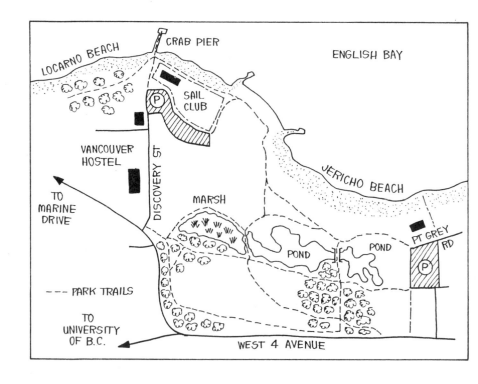

Jericho Beach Park

Blue Damselfly

KITSILANO FORESHORE

The Kitsilano Foreshore area consists mainly of the intertidal zone and low cliffs bordering the shore north of Point Grey Road in Vancouver from about Trafalgar Street on the east, to about Alma Street on the west.

Kitsilano Foreshore is not designated parkland, but is accessible from many locations. The Vancouver Park Board has agreed to consider preserving it from future development, at the prompting of neighbourhood groups. This area remains one of the few Vancouver beaches with a natural habitat for intertidal life.

Natural history highlights of the Kitsilano Foreshore include many species of birds, invertebrate wildlife, and fossiliferous bedrock. Two birding booklets, both featuring 69 bird species: *Birds Seen on the Point Grey Foreshore* (a checklist by Joe Denham and Dick Cannings), and *A Seasonal Guide to Birds of the Point Grey Foreshore* (by Henry Davis) are available from the Point Grey Natural Foreshore and Waterfowl Sanctuary Protective Society (3644 W. 16th Avenue, Vancouver, B.C. V6R 3B8).

The Kitsilano Foreshore area is home to an abundant intertidal life, in spite of proximity to a big city. Purple starfish are visible at low tide, along with two kinds of barnacles, mussels, oysters, whelks, and four types of crabs among the seaweed. The tiny purple shore crab (*Hemigrapsus sp.* - up to 4 cm) takes on camouflage patterns that resemble actual local rock types such as brownish sandstone, speckled granite, red brick or jasper, or white shell-colour. Seaweed types include brown rockweed and green sea lettuce.

Forming the structure that supports all this sea life are the gently southerly-dipping layers of Tertiary sedimentary bedrock (in age 24 to 58 million years ago). Here the Kitsilano Formation consists of interbedded sandstone, siltstone, and shale, with minor coal seams and poorly-preserved plant fossils. These rocks are similar to those in Kanaka Creek regional park, and in Stanley Park. These sediments were deposited in a low coastal river delta environment. The shaly layers contain carbonized plant fossils, which look like thin black impressions of leaves and sticks. Some thin (1 -2 cm) coal seams (compressed fossil tree trunks and branches) are exposed on the beach surface at low tide. Leaf impressions found are similar to modern trees such as alder, cedars, and the redwood Metasequoia.

Best Time to Visit: Kitsilano Foreshore is at low tide during the day in the summer, especially in June when the tides are very low; however, it is a fascinating and educational beach to visit at any time. Please do not disturb the natural inhabitants of the beach.

Bus Service: It is easily accessible from the #22 Macdonald buses, with convenient stops on Point Grey Road at Trafalgar Street or Macdonald Street. It is only four blocks north of 4th Avenue as well, so accessible also by a #4 Fourth-Blanca UBC/Powell or #7 Dunbar/Nanaimo bus.

Hazards: Watch out for incoming tide. Check the daily newspaper for tide times.

Shore Crab Suit

MUSQUEAM PARK

Though Musqueam Park is quite small, it is also an access point to the Blenheim Flats and Southlands areas. Walking trails access "the flats" and the North Arm of the Fraser River. Both coniferous and deciduous forest habitats are present. Musqueam Creek and other watercourses pass through this area which is rich in bird life and contains a nice variety of wildflowers in season.

Best Time to Visit: *Birds* - all year but a little "quiet" during July and August. *Flowers* - late April to mid June.

Bus Service: The #41 UBC (west along 41st Avenue). Note: sometimes this bus is signed 41st to Crown. Get off at Crown Street, just before entry to Pacific Spirit Regional Park. Bus travel time is 10 minutes from 41st and Granville.

Access: From the bus stop walk south along Crown Street a short 1/2 block and cross Southwest Marine Drive. Musqueam Park is to your right   (See map on page 30).   If you head straight into the park about 100 m (i.e. in a southwesterly direction), you will pick up a trail along the bank of Musqueam Creek. Following this to your left (downstream), will bring you back to Crown Street. A short distance south will be entrances to a number of trails and bridle paths both to your left and right.

All these trails and pathways are of interest. A nice western redcedar/western hemlock forest is located along the south bank of Musqueam Creek upstream from Crown. Downstream along the bridle path the forest is largely of red alder with an understorey of salmonberry and skunk cabbage.

Hazards: Sections of trails may be muddy. Watch out for cyclists and horses. This is a bridle path.

Skunk Cabbage

PACIFIC SPIRIT REGIONAL PARK

This large, 720 ha (1200 acre) regional park, in the University Endowment Lands adjacent to the University of British Columbia, is criss-crossed by 50 km of trails. The park is predominantly covered by second growth forest, and since logging occurred at various times between 40 and 100 years ago there are older coniferous forests with Douglas-fir, cedar and hemlock, and younger stands of red alder, with the occasional large bigleaf maple. The seepage slopes north of Southwest Marine Drive contain some fine Sitka spruce - now an infrequent tree in the Lower Mainland.

The foreshore edge of the Point Grey peninsula is also included in the park, and contains the clothing-optional Wreck Beach, with its steep sand cliffs. The rare narrow-leaf cattail grows in a strip of estuarine marsh along the North Arm of the Fraser River.

Maps and information are available from the GVRD park office, 4915 West 16th Avenue, tel: 224-5739, open weekdays from 8 am to 4 pm. *An Illustrated Flora of the University Endowment Lands* by Straley and Harrison, gives a good account of the plants growing in the park.

Best time to visit: All year. Good fruiting of mushrooms during the fall rains.
Flowers - during April, May, and June - best along sunlit edges of roads and broad trails.

Bus Service: The #10 UBC (west along 10th Ave.). Get off at Blanca St., at UBC gates. #41 UBC (west along 41st Ave.). Get off at Crown St. Access is also possible via #25 U.B.C. (west along 16th Ave.), which stops near the park office, another possible access point, and #42 Spanish Banks. For access to the foreshore get off the #42 Spanish Banks at Chancellor Blvd. and Newton Cres., opposite the Vancouver School of Theology. This is an infrequent bus - once an hour, and not on Sunday. Last bus is between 6 to 7 pm. Bus travel times: #10, 15 to 20 minutes from Broadway and Granville. #41, 10 minutes from 41st and Granville. #42, 10 minutes from 10th and Alma.

Access: From 10th and Blanca, walk south on Blanca to the trailhead at 12th and Blanca. From 41st and Crown, walk west one block to the northwest corner of Camosun Street, and Southwest Marine Drive, where the trail begins. For beach access walk west on Chancellor from Newton Cr., for 3 min., to the intersection of

23

Trail #3 to Tower Beach. There are many other trail access points along the park perimeter. Park users are required to stay on the trails to lessen environmental impact.

Hazards: Most of the trails are also used by horses and bicycles, and a few cyclists ride fast and recklessly. Trails can be muddy in wet weather. If visiting beach areas take very careful note of the tides, as it is easy to get trapped against the sand cliffs.

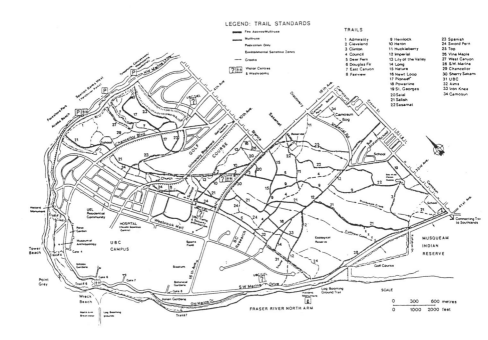

Trails in Pacific Spirit Regional Park

QUEEN ELIZABETH PARK

Queen Elizabeth Park occupies an area of 49 ha (121 ac) in the centre of Vancouver. At 153 m (500 ft), it is the highest point in the city. It is a multi-use park with tennis courts, a pitch-and-putt, bowling green, restaurant and conservatory.

Canada's first civic arboretum occupies 20 ha (50 ac) on the Park's west side. Designed by the late William Livingston the Arboretum contains one of the best collections of trees in the city. The planting is informal, with emphasis on the aesthetic value of the trees and the creation of pleasant walks and scenic views. The beautiful Quarry Gardens are located in the heart of the Arboretum in two old quarries which once supplied rock for city streets. The rock is andesite, a type of volcanic rock which is also found at Prospect Point in Stanley Park and Sentinel Hill in West Vancouver.

The Bloedel Conservatory at the top of the hill contains a selection of plants from tropical, subtropical and desert regions. About 100 small birds representing 36 species from Africa, China, South America, Indonesia and Australia fly freely about in the Conservatory. There are a few macaws and cockatoos. Japanese koi fish can be seen in the fresh water pond. (See page 9)

Queen Elizabeth park is well known to birders as one of the best spots in Vancouver to see migrating flycatchers, vireos, warblers and other passerines. In winter, Black-capped Chickadees, Ruby-crowned Kinglets, American Robins, Rufous-sided Towhees, Song Sparrows, Dark-eyed Juncos, and Bushtits are common.

Best Time to Visit: Trees — all year. Flowers — Spring and Summer
                                    Birds — Spring

Bus Service: #15 Cambie/Downtown; Southbound buses stop at 29th, 31st, and 33rd Avenues; Northbound buses stop at 30th and 33rd. #3 Main/Robson; Northbound and Southbound buses stop at 33rd and 36th. Walk west 2 blocks to get to the Park. Bus Travel Time: 5 minutes from 41st and Cambie or 41st and Main; 10 minutes from downtown (Granville and Georgia).

Facilities: Washrooms located at top of hill and at entrance to pitch-and-putt. Excellent small cafeteria with sandwiches, cookies and muffins located just below Seasons in the Park Restaurant.

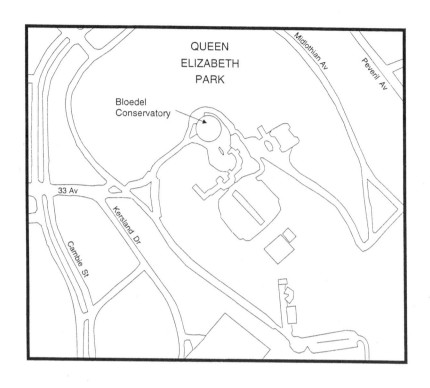

Queen Elizabeth Park and Bloedel Conservatory

Spider's web in the morning

RENFREW RAVINE

The largest urban watershed within the Vancouver and Burnaby region is the Still Creek-Burnaby Lake-Deer Lake-Brunette River System. It originates in a small lake in Central Park and ends in the Sapperton neighbourhood of New Westminster, close to the location where the first Europeans to come to the area established a military settlement. Still Creek is the waterway connecting Central and Deer Lakes. The creek is now underground for much of its length through the city. However, one point at which it is still visible is in Renfrew Ravine.

Renfrew Ravine extends north from 29th Avenue to 22nd Avenue just west of Atlin and Renfrew Streets. There is a trail along the top following the eastern edge of the ravine. The main entrance to the dirt trail following the creek along the floor of the ravine is at the corner of the Boyd Diversion and Renfrew, diagonally across from the Collingwood Community Centre.

Renfrew Ravine is one of the 14 ravines which remain in Vancouver. There used to be hundreds of ravines in Vancouver at one time but they are almost all now contained in culverts and covered over. Renfrew Ravine is a reminder of the appearance of the original landscape in Vancouver before urban development. Ravines are valued assets in the communities in which they occur. These treed environments help to buffer the noise of traffic, cool the neighbourhood on a hot day, and offer warm colours to soften the sterile vistas of roads, cars and houses. They are also sanctuaries where people and wildlife can occasionally seek refuge. Renfrew Ravine has been the focus of environmental enhancement projects by groups such as the Collingwood Neighbourhood House and the Vancouver Natural History Society.

The ravine has a small forest of bigleaf maple, alder, Douglas-fir and western redcedar. Some of the bigleaf maple are quite large. Dull Oregon grape, salal, sword fern and lady fern cover the forest floor. Vine maple, red elderberry and salmonberry are the common shrubs. There are large patches of European blackberry at many places along the forest edge.

Renfrew Ravine offers a small haven for wildlife and is a good place to go birdwatching. The Rufous-sided Towhee and Winter Wren find refuge here. Warblers, chickadees, juncos, and other birds travel through here in flocks, feeding on the rich supplies of insects and berries. The Douglas squirrel lives here, and coyotes and raccoons hide in the forest or travel through on their way to another part of the city.

Renfrew Ravine also offers us a good place to escape the hustle and bustle of the city. Once in the ravine you are surrounded by walls of vegetation which dominate your field of view. The ravine is a quiet place because the sounds of traffic are muted by the trees and ravine walls.

Best Time to Visit: The plants in the ravine can best be seen from March-October. Trails in the winter months can be somewhat muddy.

Bus Service: Renfrew Ravine can be reached in a 5 minute walk from the 29th Avenue SkyTrain station. Travel time is about 15 minutes from the Granville Street SkyTrain station.

Access: From the station walk north along Atlin Street to Renfrew, and then along Renfrew to the Boyd Diversion just before 22nd Avenue where the main trail enters into the ravine.

Hazards: The dirt trail of the ravine is slippery in the rain. It is dangerous to leave the trail to scramble up the steep slopes of the ravine itself. The water in Still Creek is polluted because of combined sewers in the area.

Location of Renfrew Ravine

Douglas-fir

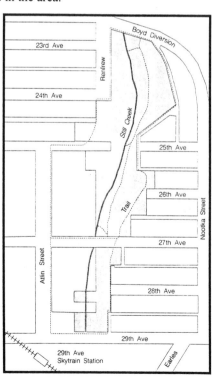

28

SOUTHLANDS

The Southlands area, around the south end of Blenheim Street, is unusual for Vancouver in that it still retains a semi-rural character, with horses, stables, and bridle paths. There are pleasant views across the North Arm of the Fraser River to Sea Island.

Access: Walk south on Blenheim Street, at first with houses to the east, and a golf course to the west, for 15 minutes. At the end of Blenheim Street a bridle and foot path, blocked by four yellow posts, goes westwards. This path at first runs parallel with Celtic Slough, but soon follows the North Arm of the Fraser River, along the south side of the Point Grey Golf Course. The path then turns north, and follows a dike along the east side of a large drainage ditch, eventually coming to the south end of Crown Street. A short distance north on Crown a trail begins which allows one to continue on to Musqueam and Pacific Spirit Parks. (See pages 21 and 23) Instead of turning north beside the ditch, it is possible to continue along the edge of the Musqueam Golf Course. There is a private property sign here, but access is not restricted at the present time. This trail eventually reaches a wide channel, the banks of which support black hawthorn, and Pacific crab apple trees. A pleasant side trip is also available a block or so north of 51st Avenue where small trails enter the deciduous woods of the Musqueam Marsh Nature Park.

Bus Service: #49 Dunbar UBC (west via 49th Avenue, and Southwest Marine Drive). Get off at Southwest Marine and Blenheim Street. Bus travel time is 10 minutes from 49th and Granville.

Best Time to Visit: All year.

Hazards: Watch for stray golf balls. These paths are also used by horses and bicycles, and some can be muddy in wet weather. Entry to the Musqueam Band property to the west is not allowed without permission.

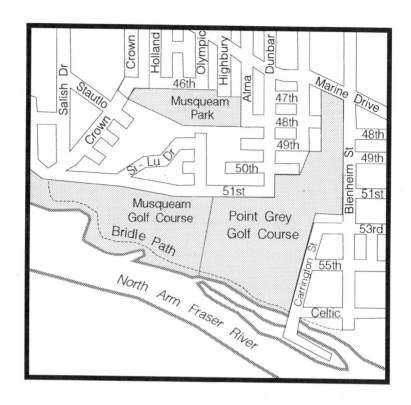

Location of Musqueam Park

Salmonberry

STANLEY PARK

Stanley Park is the green heart of the City of Vancouver. Backed by the dense highrises of the West End it forms a peninsula which juts out into Burrard Inlet, creating the "First Narrows" and protecting the Vancouver harbour. Encompassed within its 400 ha (1000 ac) are marine foreshore, coniferous forest, lakes, streams and formal gardens as well as picnic areas and playgrounds. It is home to the famous Vancouver Aquarium and the Nature House at Lost Lagoon.

Below its green cover the peninsula consists of till, clay and silt, deposited by retreating glaciers over 10,000 years ago, and underlying soft sedimentary rock. Two of Stanley Park's major landmarks, the legendary Siwash Rock and Prospect Point, were formed about 35 million years ago when upthrusting black magma split the older sedimentary rock, leaving behind these substantial promontories.

The 8.8 km (6 mi) seawall from English Bay on the west to Lost Lagoon and Coal Harbour on the east provides access to the marine foreshore. Summer low tides expose seastars, chitons, anemones, clams, limpets, crabs and seaweeds. Gulls and crows feed on the bounty, and in winter rafts of diving and dabbling ducks, grebes, loons, cormorants and alcids can be seen off shore.

The forest covering most of the park belongs to the Drier Maritime subzone of the Coastal Western Hemlock zone, and consists primarily of western redcedar, western hemlock and Douglas-fir with a rich understory of salmonberry, vine maple, salal, and many ferns, mosses and fungi. Despite logging in the 1800's and Typhoon Frieda in 1962, there are good examples of old-growth forest between Pipeline and Tunnel Roads.

More than 230 species of birds have been seen in the park. Stands of large bigleaf maple and red alder scattered throughout the park provide the best opportunities for seeing smaller birds as they migrate through in spring and fall. Lost Lagoon in winter is a "must see" with thousands of wintering waterfowl while Beaver Lake attracts warblers and flycatchers in June and July. Bald Eagles nest in the park and there is an active Great Blue Heron rookery near the Aquarium.

The variety of native mammals and amphibians has decreased dramatically over the years however shy coyotes still roam the park, over-fed raccoons and skunks may appear anywhere, and Douglas squirrels are surviving against the eastern greys. Seals and sealions can be seen in English Bay or basking on rocks offshore.

In the lakes and streams salamanders, frogs, toads, turtles and garter snakes may be found.

There are a number of beautiful and interesting gardens on the south side of Stanley Park. The Rose Garden and the Perennial Garden are just to the east of the causeway. From early spring to late summer, roses, cherries, magnolias, rhododendrons, spring bulbs, summer annuals, and large beds bursting with perennials make this one of the most colourful spots in the Park.

The small formal garden in front of the Dining Pavilion is a bright and cheerful garden with lots of colour and the Garden of Remembrance, located in a shady area behind the Dining Pavilion is a place for quiet contemplation. There is a very nice woodland garden around the pitch-and-putt on the west side of the Park. Here, cherries, magnolias and rhododendrons put on an impressive floral display in the spring. In 1989 it was named the Ted and Mary Greig Rhododendron Garden and contains hundreds of hybrid rhododendrons from the Greig collection.

Bus Service: #11 Stanley Park stops at the park entrance next to Lost Lagoon, and during July and August the #52 Around the Park bus runs during daylight hours.

Best Time to Visit: All year.

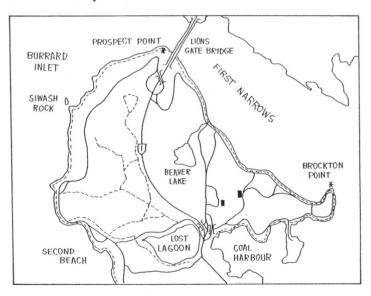

Stanley Park

An excellent review of nature in the park can be found in *The Natural History of Stanley Park*, by the Vancouver Natural History Society. This is available at The Nature House, tel. 257-8544.

UNIVERSITY OF BRITISH COLUMBIA BOTANICAL GARDEN

The University of British Columbia Botanical Garden occupies 24 ha (60 ac) in the southwest corner of the campus. In the David C. Lam Asian Garden native conifers provide shelter for an outstanding collection of trees, shrubs, and climbing plants. The rhododendron and magnolia collections are among the best to be found anywhere. The E.H. Lohbrunner Alpine Garden occupies 1 ha on a sunny west-facing slope. It is divided geographically, with separate sections for Australia, Europe, North America, South America, Africa Asia and Asia Minor. The BC Native Garden contains a large number of plants from a variety of habitats (coastal forest, bog, marsh, dry interior) and is an excellent place to begin a study of our native flora. The Physick Garden is a charming little garden containing medicinal plants used in western medicine since ancient times. Information labels describing the uses of the plants make fascinating reading. The Winter Garden contains a surprisingly large number of plants which flower in the winter months, and some of these are among the most fragrant in the Garden. Others have been selected for their attractive fruit or foliage. The beautiful Perennial Borders are filled with plants which have been carefully chosen for their colour, texture, size, and form. The Food Garden demonstrates the culture of a variety of fruits and vegetables suitable for the home garden.

The Garden is an excellent place for bird watching. Bald Eagles are common, especially in winter. The Asian Garden is home to a pair of Great Horned Owls. Killdeer lay their eggs on gravel in the Alpine Garden. Brewer's Blackbirds, Brown-headed Cowbirds, American Goldfinches, and White-crowned Sparrows are common in the open, middle area of the Garden. Rufous Hummingbirds are attracted to the exotic flowers in the Garden. Over 60 species of birds have been recorded for the Native Garden.

Best Time to Visit: *Flowers:* Asian Garden — January - May. Perennial Borders — late Spring - Summer. Winter Garden — January - March
Birds: Mid-May, September

The UBC Botanical Garden is at 6804 SW Marine Drive, at the corner of SW Marine Drive and West Mall.

Bus Service: #42 Chancellor - Monday to Saturday - hourly service. Travel time: 16 minutes from Alma at 10th. Route terminates at the Garden .

The following buses take you within easy walking distance of the Botanical Garden:

#4,9,10,25,41 UBC to University Loop. Walk 2 blocks west on University Boulevard then south on West Mall to SW Marine Drive. Walking time: 20 minutes.

#25 UBC to Westbrook Mall at 16th Avenue. Walk southwest on 16th Avenue to SW Marine Drive, then northwest one block to the Garden. Walking time: 15 minutes.

#41 UBC to 16th Avenue at SW Marine Drive. Walk northwest one block. Walking time: 5 minutes.

Swamp Gentian

VANDUSEN BOTANICAL GARDEN

The VanDusen Botanical Garden occupies 22 ha (35 ac) on what was the old Shaughnessy golf course. Designed by the late William Livingston, this beautiful garden contains a unique and valuable collection of over 6,500 kinds of plants. In the formal area near the Garden Pavilion there are a number of small gardens, including a Children's Garden, Rock Garden, Fragrance Garden and Rose Garden.

The Rhododendron Walk on the south side of the Garden contains a large collection of hybrid rhododendrons. The Heather Garden is located in the centre of the Garden and is meant to evoke the bleak moorlands of Northern Europe. There is a traditional perennial border in the Perennials and Grasses area, while in the Alma VanDusen Garden perennials are planted in an open meadow design. A large part of the collection is arranged by geographic area, with separate gardens containing Western North American, Eastern North American, Southern Hemisphere, Mediterranean and Sino-Himalayan flora. The Sino-Himalayan Garden is designed to simulate the humid steep-sided wooded valleys of montane temperate China. It contains an outstanding collection of rhododendron species. The Western North American Garden is planted around a simulated glacial ravine, complete with riverbed. Most plants are labelled for easy identification. Native plants in the Medicinal Plant Collection in the Heritage Garden are provided with information labels describing aboriginal and modern uses.

The soil in the Garden is the same glacial till that underlies most of Vancouver. A number of different types of rocks, most of local origin, have been used for various purposes. Sandstone, excavated from various sites in Vancouver, has been used extensively, especially in the streams, waterfalls, and lakes. The limestone in the Rock Garden and the metamorphic granite conglomerate in the simulated glacial ravine in the Western North American Garden come from the North Shore. The rounded stones in the south arm of the "river" in the glacial ravine come from the Capilano River. The volcanic rock (basalt - andesite) used to make the stone shelter in the Heather Garden is from Queen Elizabeth Park. The Grotto on the east side of the Heather Garden is made of black basalt conglomerate from the False Creek area. The andesite for the wall in the Perennials and Grasses area is from Haddington Island near Alert Bay. This is the same material that was used for the exterior of the legislative building in Victoria. Nephrite jade from northern BC was used to make the drinking fountain, the pedestal of the sun dial, and the sculpture in the reflecting pool. The lava rocks in the Stone Garden are from a quarry near Reno, Nevada.

A pamphlet entitled: *The Birds of the VanDusen Botanical Garden,* is available at the shop. A checklist at the back lists 62 of the commoner species seen in the Garden.

Best Time to Visit: spring and summer

Bus Service: #17 Oak/Downtown.   Bus Travel Time: 5 minutes from 41st and Oak, 30 minutes from downtown

Access: Entrance is at 37th Avenue and Oak.   The garden is open every day. There is an entrance fee, a guidebook is on sale, there is a free map, and there are self-guided and guided tours.   Wheelchairs are available, and volunteer-driven electric carts take visitors around the Garden in summer.

Great Blue Heron

American Coot and chick

Western Hemlock

BURNABY MOUNTAIN

Over twice the size of Stanley Park, the forested area on Burnaby Mountain is within easy reach of most places in the Lower Mainland. The mountain is a large, unofficial wildlife sanctuary, and because Simon Fraser University is located on top of the mountain, bus service is excellent.

Trail maps are usually available at the gas station. Standing on the road, facing the station, you will see mountains to the north. Walk to the right (east), to the edge of the gas station property where you will see a trail running down into the forest. Follow this trail (Shell Trail) until you come to the T-intersection. This is Joe's Trail.

At this point you have two options: you can go left through the forest to Burnaby Mountain Park (the trail here is called Perimeter Trail), an open park area with magnificent views and large grassy spaces (Route A), or you can turn right along Joe's Trail which will take you further into the forest towards other connecting trails (Route B).

Route A: This gently-sloping trail winds through second-growth forest for 1/2 km. Here you will find bigleaf maple, alder and the shade-tolerant hemlock. Remnants of past logging, such as old cedar stumps and fallen "nurse logs", are still visible.

Keep to the right as you exit the forest and follow the fence which will lead to rewarding views of Burrard Inlet and the Coast Range Mountains. Park facilities include a children's playground, washrooms and a concession stand (in season).

Route B: Joe's Trail winds slowly down a slope for 1 km through groves of maples and hemlocks. In spring there are lovely beds of trilliums with bleeding hearts lining the trail. In summer there is cool shade and a wide variety of songbirds such as Rufous-sided Towhee, Winter Wren and Swainson's Thrush. In fall the trail is covered with golden maple leaves. In winter, if it snows, you can see the tracks of black-tailed deer, coyotes and snowshoe hares.

Joe's Trail ends at Cardiac Hill Trail. If you turn right the trail will lead you up a steep incline to the university. If you turn left the trail will lead down to the base of the mountain.

Bus Service: Take any bus bound for Simon Fraser University and get off at the main bus stop.

Access: Walk straight ahead (north) from the bus stop, turn left, and within a minute you will arrive at the campus gas station (ask the bus driver for directions if you are unsure). This is the starting point.

Hazards: There may be muddy sections on trails after heavy rains. Watch for mountain bikes on steep sections. Keep away from cliffs and ravine edges.

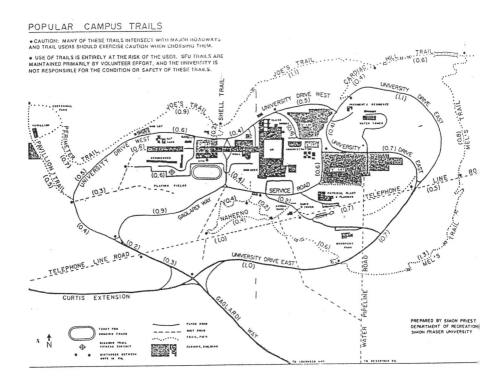

POPULAR CAMPUS TRAILS

Trails on Burnaby Mountain

BURNABY LAKE AND DEER LAKE

Burnaby Lake Regional Nature Park and Deer Lake Park are two outstanding natural areas in an urban setting. They offer an escape from the city within the city and provide the opportunity to enjoy beautiful walks and hikes and a wide variety of plants, animals, birds, reptiles and invertebrates. They are places to enjoy the passing of the seasons, whether reflected in the seasonally changing bird life, or in the forests. Marshes, rivers and fields make up the area. Both parks are located in what is known locally as Burnaby's central valley and are part of the ecologically very important Burnaby Lake/Brunette River watershed.

The land now occupied by the parks was extensively logged around the turn of the century, and walking the many forest trails, one can see much evidence of this activity. Large western redcedar stumps with the springboard holes still visible are found throughout the forested areas. Just west of the Nature House at Burnaby Lake, the remnants of a sawmill can be identified from the large mound of sawdust and wood waste now being colonized by birch trees.

The two parks occupy an area dominated by lowland, second-growth, mixed forest habitat which, in both cases, forms the larger part of the lands surrounding the lakes. Burnaby Lake has fairly extensive marshes around most of its shoreline and these reach their greatest extent at its eastern end where the outlet to the lake becomes the Brunette River, which then flows to the Fraser River.

While Burnaby Lake has extensive marshland, Deer Lake has limited habitat of this kind. But what it lacks in marshland it makes up for in the fairly extensive area of rough grassland at its western end. Close to the shore at the lake's northwest corner is a small remnant sphagnum bog.

This modest but interesting variety of habitats - forests, marshland, bogs, rough meadow/grassland and freshwater streams and lakes along with the gardens and mowed playing fields - is the basis for the variety of birds and other wildlife that occupy the parks and is so much a part of their attraction. Over 200 species of birds, 13 species of fish, 16 species of reptiles and amphibians, 31 species of mammals and over 200 species of plants are recorded in these two parks.

The two parks are joined by Deer Lake Creek which flows into Burnaby Lake from the south. This stream is being enhanced to support larger numbers of spawning coho salmon, and in common with many of the other watercourses in the watershed such as Stoney Creek and the Brunette River, is providing a model for the rehabilitation and preservation of urban streams to support salmon, steelhead and cutthroat trout.

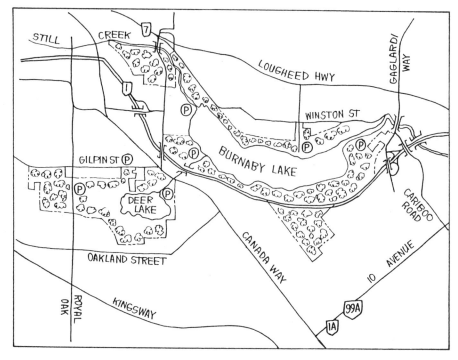

Burnaby Lake and Deer Lake

For Burnaby Lake the main points of access are:

1.   The Burnaby Lake Sports Complex at the junction of Kensington Ave and Sprott St at the west end of the park. Access here leads to the main trail which circles the lake for approximately a 10 km walk and can be taken in either direction. Buses to this location are: #110 and #144 from Metrotown Station.

2.   The foot of Piper Ave off Government Rd is probably the most popular access to the park. Access here takes you directly to the Piper Ave spit which is a popular place to feed birds and of course it provides access to the main lake trail. A bus to this location is the #110 from Lougheed Mall.

3.   At the east end of the park the Avalon Ave entrance off Cariboo Rd brings you to the vicinity of the Cariboo Dam crossing of the Brunette River. This access

also takes you to the equestrian centre and the trails at this end of the lake are the most likely places to meet horses and riders on your walks. The #101 bus to this location originates at Lougheed Mall.

For Deer Lake the main points of access are:

1.   At the foot of the Royal Oak Ave hill immediately to the south of Deer Lake Parkway. This entrance takes you into the more natural parts of the park and the heritage meadow (an important wildlife area) which borders the western end of the lake. There are many trails to take here. Some circle the meadow, others circle the lake and others give access to the forested areas of the park. The bus to this location is the #130 from Metrotown.

2.   Sperling Ave just south of Canada Way. This easternmost part of the park has a beach and children's playground and is among the most developed part of the park. It provides good views of the whole lake and access to the lakeshore trail is easy here. From this location one can walk to the more natural areas of the park by generally heading west. The buses #131 and #132 go close to this location - get off at the corner of Burris St and Buckingham Ave and walk west down Buckingham to the park.

3.   Off Deer Lake Drive immediately to the south of Canada Way. This area is dominated by the new Shadbolt Centre for the Arts and the James Cowan Theatre complexes. While highly developed, easy access is gained to the lakeshore trail, and pleasant walks in Spring can be taken through Burnaby's spectacular rhododendron garden that is in this area. Any buses to Burnaby's City Hall will get you close - the #s 110, 120, 131, 132, 144. Get off at City Hall and walk east along Deer Lake Ave.

Green Frog

4.   Coming from Oakland St from the north foot of Brandford Ave or from Baffin Pl. These two access points take you into the steep, forested southern parts of the park. The access off Brantford is informal and connects to some of the more rugged trails in the park. The access from Baffin Pl leads to a well developed trail which soon descends through the forest bringing you to the meadow and lakeshore trails. Buses to these locations are the same as to the recreation park mentioned above. Walk past the park to the stairs up the hill. At the top of the stairs, take a right onto Haszard St and look for trails into the park along the park's edge.

Note: At time of going to press the southern part of the lakeshore trail at Deer Lake is incomplete. The properties on the south shore of the lake have been acquired by the City of Burnaby and the planning process to develop an appropriate route, with minimal environmental impact, has been started. On the north side of the lake, there are small areas of the lakeshore that are still privately owned and not accessible. The trail in this area is very easy to follow and your walk can circle the lake but at places skirts the private properties.

Damselfly Nymph

BYRNE CREEK RAVINE

Byrne Creek Ravine Park is one of six large ravines along Burnaby's south slope. They were formed by erosion of the glacial till and outwash along the edges of the Burrard Peninsula on which much of Vancouver and Burnaby are located. It extends 1 km south from the Edmonds SkyTrain station at the top to Marine Drive on the bottom. The ravine is bordered by Ron McLean Park and residential homes to the west, and townhouses to the east.

Byrne Creek drains into the Fraser River and was once used by salmon as a natural spawning area. Salmon and cutthroat trout were caught here just a few decades ago. Water quality in the creek has suffered from urban runoff and storm drainage. Several large storm drains channel water into the creek from as far away as Kingsway to the north. There has been a salmonid enhancement program in Byrne Creek since the 1980s. The Vancouver Angling and Game Association and the local schools have removed much of the garbage from the creek, marked storm drains to emphasize the impact of runoff on water quality, and stocked the creek with salmon fry. The creek now contains an artificial spawning channel and spawning habitat.

The ravine is a rich ecosystem. The plant communities reflect the dramatic changes in soil moisture created by the steep slopes. The floor of the ravine is wet and rich in nutrients which leach from the slopes. A mature community of bigleaf maple follows the creek. These large trees are covered in moss and, especially during the wetter months of the year, are covered with licorice fern. The bark and moss of the trunks have a diversity of insect life. Salmonberry, red elderberry and vine maple provide excellent habitat for birds and cover over the banks of the creek to shelter salmon. Skunk cabbage and horsetail are common.

The drier slopes of the ravine have large Douglas-fir, western redcedar and western hemlock. Protected from the wind in the ravine, these trees have grown to large heights and give the impression of old growth. There are several snags in with the trees. Beneath the trees the forest floor is covered with sword and lady ferns. Along the edge at the top of the ravine are alder, birch and cherry. The ground cover contains dull Oregon grape and salal.

The ravine attracts many animals. The undersides of stones in the creek have clinging invertebrates such as stone fly nymphs. The insects and berries in the ravine are food for a wide range of birds — warblers, thrushes, woodpeckers, chickadees and even Great-blue Heron. The tall trees are used as perches by raptors; Red-tailed Hawk, Bald Eagle, and Great-horned Owl are sometimes seen. Mammals such as coyote and raccoon hunt in the ravine or use it as a wildlife corridor while travelling to various parts of the city.

Access: There are two main trails through the ravine. One is north off Marine Drive about 100 m east of Byrne Road. The entrance is well marked by a sign. The trail is well constructed, about 2 m wide with a cover of gravel and is relatively gentle grade as it follows the creek. The 400 m trail ends in a staircase that leads out of the ravine to the residential area (Brynlor Drive), on the top of the slope. However, instead of going out onto the road you can follow a trail just inside the edge of the forest to the west side of the park playground.

A second trail is at the east end of the playground and enters into the forest just south of a large outdoor rink. This dirt trail immediately descends to the ravine floor and then continues about 200 m south along the creek to a large rocky spillway for a storm drain that drains from the top of the ravine at that point.

Bus Service: The #100 bus which goes between Vancouver International Airport and the New Westminster and 22nd Street SkyTrain stations stops on Marine Drive by Byrne Road, close to the trail entering into the ravine. The trail from Ron McLean Park can be reached from the Edmonds SkyTrain station. There is a path used by people living in the area to walk to the SkyTrain station which leads from the west side of the parking lot next to the station, under the guideway, and follows a fence to the park. Travel time is about 25 minutes from the Granville Street SkyTrain station, 5 minutes from New Westminster.

Best Time to Visit: The ravine can be visited year round. Most of the interesting plants are seen from March to October. The winter months from November to February can be very muddy in the ravine bottom.

Hazards: The slope of the ravine itself is quite steep and should be avoided. The dirt trail can get slippery in rain.

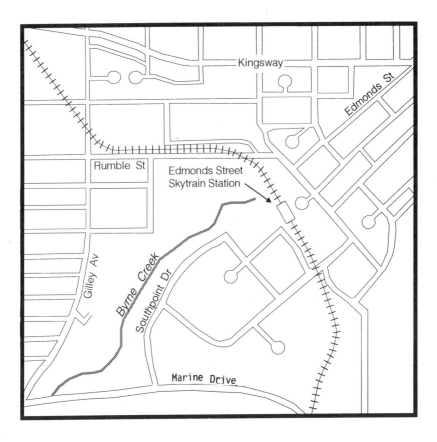

Location of Byrne Creek Ravine

Brown Creeper

Bald Eagle

CENTRAL PARK

This unique municipal park was first reserved in 1863 by the Royal Engineers as a source of masts for the British Navy. Later in the 19th century a tram line and station were established in the general area. The entire site was logged in the 1890s. There are still many large stumps remaining, remnants of the magnificent giants which used to grow here.

The park is a heavily forested area with two small lakes. Douglas-fir, western redcedar, western hemlock, vine maple, paper birch and red elderberry are all common. There are also many common shrubs: salmonberry, thimbleberry, and huckleberry. Along the edge of Swangard Stadium is the European honeysuckle with its red and yellow flowers. The forests attract the Douglas squirrel, Downy Woodpecker, Rufous-sided Towhee, and numerous sparrows and finches.

The two small artificial lakes are called Upper Lake and Lower Lake and are joined by a stream. Upper Lake contains crayfish, three-spined sticklebacks and a rich supply of zooplankton such as Daphnia and Cyclops. Lower Lake contains many Brown Bullhead catfish. Many waterfowl such as Canada Geese and Mallards are attracted to the lakes.

In addition to the nearly 900 ha (2250 acres)of natural habitat, Central Park also has a playground (including equipment for disabled children), lawn bowling, tennis courts, pitch-and-putt golf, an outdoor pool, a picnic area, baseball diamonds, jogging and a fitness loop. It is wheelchair accessible with wide, well-maintained paths.

Access: A trail enters the park immediately next to the Patterson SkyTrain station.

Bus Service: The SkyTrain will take you directly to the park. Get off at the Patterson Station. The park is at the corner of Kingsway and Boundary so any Kingsway bus will also get you there.

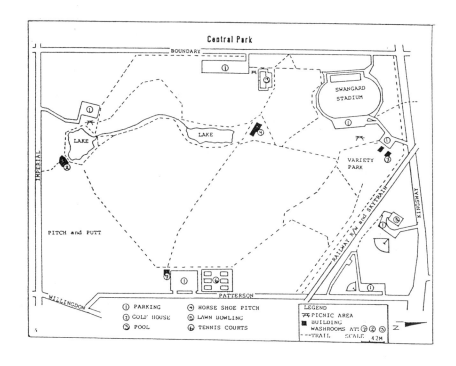

Central Park

Stonefly Nymph

ROBERT BURNABY PARK

This is a jewel of a municipal park which is part of the Burnaby Lake-Brunette River watershed. The natural habitat occurs primarily in several ravines which begin along 4th Street to the west. The largest of these runs from 4th Street through the entire length of the park to the Trans Canada Highway. There is a trail that follows its upper bank and then descends down into the floor of the ravine. At the mouth of the ravine the stream bank is reinforced by attractive stone walls.

The forest is primarily second growth of bigleaf maple, alder and vine maple with some Douglas-fir and redcedar. The ground on the slopes of the ravines is covered with ferns (especially sword ferns), foam flower, large-leaved avens and bleeding heart. The wetter habitat adjacent to the stream contains skunk cabbage.

The protected ravine environment and the proximity of the park to Burnaby Lake Regional Park make this area rich with wildlife. Many of the local songbirds, hawks and owls are found here. Coyotes make their way into the park along connecting corridors of utility rights-of-way.

In addition to over 200 ha (500 acres) of natural habitat, Robert Burnaby Park also has a children's playground, tennis courts, an outdoor pool, and a sports field. In the winter the slope next to the playground is a popular spot for tobogganing,

Access: The park is bounded by 4th Street to the west, Hill Avenue to the east, and 19th and 20th Avenues to the south. There are about 2.5 km of trails which arise from each of these roads. The best natural history walks begin from the trails along 4th Street on either side of the sports field at the end of Elwell Street.

Bus Service: The #106 from the Edmonds SkyTrain Station travels closest to this area. Depending on the time and day the bus runs about every 10-20 minutes. Get off at the corner of 19th Avenue and 6th Street, a 10 minute ride from the SkyTrain station. Walk east two blocks to the park.

Hazards: The ravine slopes are very steep. Trails can be slippery when wet.

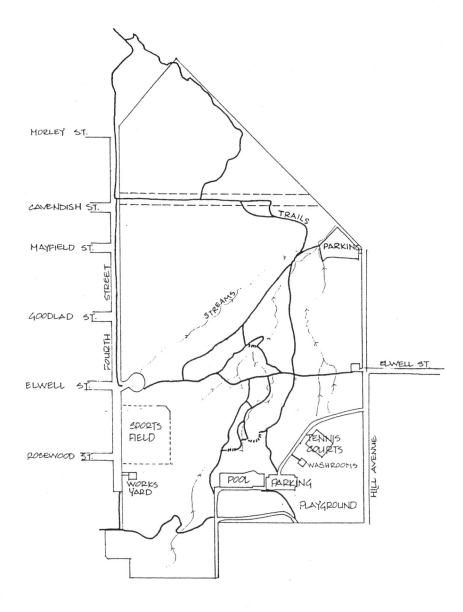

Robert Burnaby Park

COQUITLAM

Easter Lily

Horsetail

MUNDY PARK

Mundy Park is the largest municipal park in Coquitlam. It has easy access, wide, well-maintained trails and excellent diversity of flora and fauna. It offers a variety of habitats including wetlands, a bog, coniferous forest and cultivated grass.

The park has a large forested area comprised of Douglas-fir, western redcedar, western hemlock, white birch and vine maple. The forest floor consists of familiar west coast species such as ferns, salmonberry, huckleberry, salal and mosses. The vegetation of the wetland and bog areas (sedges, cattails, Labrador tea, shore pine) provides an interesting contrast.

Mundy Park is a welcome refuge for many birds, raccoons, squirrels and bull-frogs. There is an excellent variety of bird species which frequent the park all year round. Some of the species you may encounter include Pileated Woodpeckers, Steller's Jays, Black-capped Chickadees, Brown Creepers, juncos, wrens, and sparrows.

Access: Mundy Park is a pleasant and accessible place to enjoy the outdoors. The terrain is quite level and safe for most people. It is a good family park with some amenities like an outdoor swimming pool, lacrosse box, picnic tables, and baseball diamond. Its large area and diversity make it an interesting and worthwhile place to visit year round.

Bus Service: You can reach Mundy Park by taking the #154 Lougheed Mall from the 22nd Street SkyTrain station and getting off at Hillcrest Avenue (main park entrance). Travel time is about 40 minutes.

The #143 SFU/Coquitlam Centre and #151 Vancouver/Port Coquitlam Centre travel along Como Lake Road where there is access to the park at a well-marked trail near Baker Drive. The #143 runs at commuter times Monday to Friday. Approximate time from SFU to the park is 30 minutes.

The schedule for the #151 varies during the week. It is best to check a current bus timetable for routes and schedules. If you come from Vancouver the travel time is about an hour.

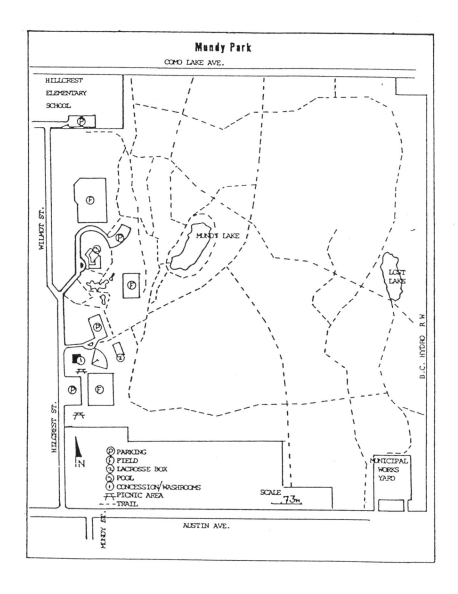

Mundy Park

Double-crested Cormorants

Bleeding Heart

AMBLESIDE PARK

Although Ambleside Park is manicured and much used, this small 24 ha (60 ac) urban park provides a variety of bird habitats. Here one has access to the mouth of the Capilano River with its loafing gulls, a small brackish marsh where herons and bald eagles roost, the seashore with diving waterfowl and a pond populated by dabbling ducks, all adjacent to a good (albeit shrinking) woodlot. This oasis has attracted many unusual bird species over the years and is known as a migrant trap in both spring and fall.

Birders should check the gravel bars (low tide) on both river and foreshore for uncommon species among the resting gulls and waterfowl. The paths that lead off the main trail into the woodlot allow access to the interior of this mixed deciduous and coniferous forest and expose shrubby areas open to the sun. Rocky spits that lead out beyond the shoreline provide vantage points to view open water in the harbour and the seawalk gives opportunities to look for diving waterfowl closer to shore. The pond is surrounded by brushy growth and cultivated plantings, attracting passerines, while the waterfowl on the pond may include unusual and even rare species such as Ring-necked and Tufted ducks in winter.

Walk westward towards the west end of the park at 13th Street or continue along the shoreline as far as you like. The return bus to Vancouver may be boarded anywhere along Marine Drive, which parallels the shore one block north.

Best time to Visit: Birding is worthwhile all year round while botanists may enjoy the cultivated trees and shrubs.

Bus Service: All West Vancouver buses leave Downtown Vancouver making stops along Georgia Street, pass through Stanley Park and over the Lions Gate Bridge, to enter West Vancouver. Get off at the bus stop on Marine Drive 100 m beyond Taylor Way (Park Royal Shopping Centre), the second stop after Lions Gate Bridge. Travel time is about 15 minutes from Granville and Georgia.

Access: From Marine Drive walk south along Taylor Way 150 m to the bank of the Capilano River. A path leaves the river bank, skirts the marsh, going westward to a point where it enters the woodlot, just south of the Eaton's store. Here the path widens to a trail, winding southward along the river toward Ambleside itself and the bay beyond.

Hazards: An active railway line passes through this area.

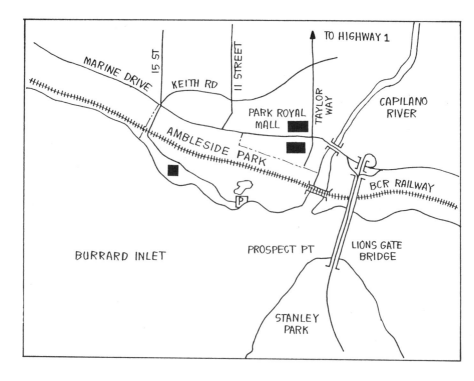

Location of Ambleside Park

Glaucous-winged Gull with Sea Star

CAPILANO RIVER REGIONAL PARK

This sliver of park follows the Capilano River from Cleveland Dam and Capilano Lake to the river mouth at Ambleside Park, some 236 m lower in elevation. The spectacular vista of The Lions with Mt. Strachan, Crown and Grouse Mountains surrounding Capilano Lake provide the backdrop. Rugged terrain with 100 year old trees, native fauna and flora, breathtaking views of the river and its deep gorge in the granite mountainside make this an excellent destination. Most of the 160 ha (400 ac) are in the upper portion with a thin strip adjacent to the river for the last third of the 7.5 km trail to the sea. A large portion of this trail follows the route of the Capilano Timber Co. Railway, 1917-1933, and remains of the flume built in the canyon to carry shingle bolts down the mountainside can still be seen. The Capilano Fish Hatchery, built in 1972, has educational displays and views of juvenile or adult salmon and, in season, returning salmon in the fish ladder. The river has been a popular destination since the 1880's because of its dramatic natural setting. Historical documentation of the past century is displayed on the Capilano Suspension Bridge property.

The upper two-thirds of the park, away from urbanization, is most interesting for the naturalist. This is largely evergreen western hemlock, Douglas-fir and western redcedar forest with deciduous red alder. Ferns, lichens and mosses are well represented. Varied Thrush, Red-breasted Sapsucker, Winter Wren, Steller's Jay, Chestnut-backed Chickadee and Pine Siskin are some common bird species. American Dippers are sometimes found on the lower river in winter.

Best Time to Visit: The park is open year round. Spring is best for forest bird watching but specialty species may be found in all seasons. May to early July is best for flowering plants and shrubs.

Bus Service: The #232 Grouse Mountain leaves Phibbs Exchange and travels via Edgemont Village to Grouse Mountain Skyride, passing Cleveland Dam and the upper park access (30 min service). From Lonsdale Quay #236 Grouse Mountain travels Capilano Road to Grouse Mountain Skyride, passing the upper park access (60 min service). From Downtown Vancouver bus #246 Highland goes through Edgemont Village (30 minute service). Transfer here to #212 Grouse Mountain in Edgemont Village or #236 Grouse Mountain on Capilano Road. (Check with your driver for your best option). During peak hours (until 9:30 a.m. weekdays), #247 Upper Capilano leaves from Downtown Vancouver via Georgia Street and travels direct to Cleveland Dam (30 minute service).

Bus travel time to the park is approximately 35 minutes from Downtown Vancouver or Phibbs Exchange, 30 minutes from Lonsdale Quay.

Access: Get off your bus at Prospect Avenue and Capilano Road (Capilano River Regional Park sign) and walk west through the parking lot toward the picnic area and Cleveland Dam. A directory map shows the many interconnecting trails that lace the upper portion of the park. The Baden-Powell trail crosses over Cleveland Dam leading to destinations west on Hollyburn Mountain or east to Grouse Mountain, Mt. Seymour, and Deep Cove. The Capilano Pacific Trail begins south or east of the picnic area (two trailheads), descends to the fish hatchery (1 km), crosses a bridge over the river and continues downward along the river canyon to the seashore. Signposts, view spots and rest areas along the route offer options for descent. Picnic facilities are found at both the dam site and fish hatchery.

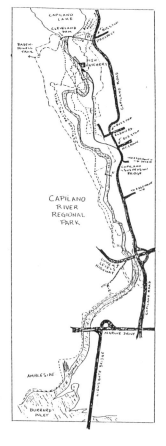

Alternate access points two-thirds of the way from the bottom (seashore) and 400 m above the Capilano Suspension Bridge lead to trails through the eastern portion of the park. Get off your bus at the junction of Capilano Road and Capilano Park Road (bus stop at Mt. Crown Street) or 200 m further (bus stop on Eldon Street) and walk into the park to the fish hatchery and information kiosk (1.2 km) where you can consider further options.

Hazards: Rugged terrain, slippery footbridges, and precipitous drops are very dangerous so caution, particularly with children, must be observed.

*Capilano River
Regional Park*

Male Blue Grouse (Coastal Form)

62

CAULFEILD PARK

Caulfeild Park is a municipal park in West Vancouver, comprising about 3.5 ha (9 ac) of waterfront east of Lighthouse Park parallel to the 4700 block of Marine Drive. A monument with an anchor commemorates Francis William Caulfeild (1843-1934), founder of the local community.

Caulfeild Park is famous as a geological field trip site because it is the most accessible place in the Lower Mainland where amphibolite grade metamorphic rocks can be observed in contact with the more dominant granodioritic rocks. There are a few outstanding outcrops showing the crosscutting relationships among several different rock types, all within the Coast Plutonic Complex. The Caulfeild gneiss is a folded amphibolite, perhaps of pre-Jurassic age (older than 208 million years ago). It was intruded by granodioritic plutonic rocks during the Cretaceous period (144 to 66.4 million years ago), such as the rocks that underlie Lighthouse Park. Several intrusive episodes have produced different types of crosscutting dykes, such as porphyritic andesite, and a pink granitic unit known as the aplite/pegmatite, as well as migmatitic features such as xenoliths and schlieren. Tiny garnets may be found in the aplite/pegmatite unit, as well as graphic texture. The crystalline rocks of Caulfeild Park show evidence of glacial rounding and smoothing, and provide a good viewpoint over English Bay.

Although a small, narrow park (extending about 100 m up from the rocky shore), Caulfeild Park hosts many types of plants. Trees include western redcedar, Douglas-fir, arbutus, maple, apple, hawthorn, weeping willow, and pine. An eclectic combination of bushes such as salal, blackberry, cherry laurel, bamboo, legumes, rose family plants, ivy, wisteria, and bracken fern provide privacy for those on the rocky shore, as well as for small wildlife and birds. The Douglas squirrel (chickaree) has been seen there.

When the tide is low, many large purple and orange starfish can be seen. Little shore crabs match the pink aplite rocks and red iron-stained granodiorite. Harbour seals may be seen swimming offshore.

Bus Service: West Vancouver bus #250 Horseshoe Bay.

Access: Get off at Piccadilly Road South, and walk down to Pilot House Road. A public beach at the eastern end of Caulfeild Park is accessible by a stairway down from Marine Drive at Piccadilly South. As there is no place to park, it is best to take public transit. Outhouses are only open in the summer.

Purple Sea Star

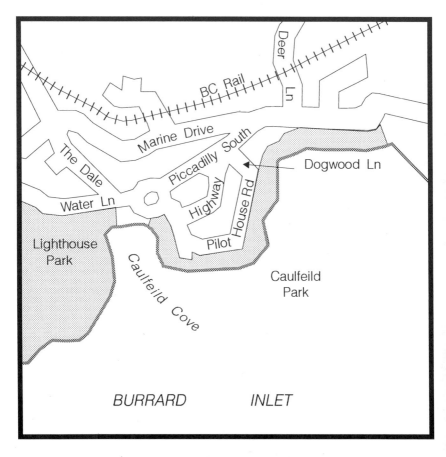

Location of Caulfeild Park

HOLLYBURN RIDGE

The slopes of Hollyburn Mountain above the British Properties, upwards of 380 m elevation, offer a network of trails and fire access roads through dense coastal forest. These tracks, originally logging roads, date from 1870 to the first decades of this century. Many old growth trees remain within the second growth, as well as snags and stumps, showing a natural succession and regeneration of the forest following the disturbances of logging and two major fires (1910 and 1916). Evidence of the early logging methods are still visible. Open spaces give spectacular views of harbour and city. The trails can be enjoyed in short sections or followed to the heights of the mountain itself (1,325m). Many small lakes and bogs, plus numerous creeks and waterfalls, make ideal destination points. While birdlife and wildflowers are present in these deeply wooded areas, it is the forest itself with its cool damp air, earthy smells and the weighty presence of giant trees that reward the naturalist who journeys to this mountainside overlooking Vancouver.

This is western hemlock and Douglas-fir forest with many fine examples of these and other coniferous and deciduous trees such as western redcedar, amabilis fir, red alder and bigleaf maple. Flowering shrubs include huckleberry, blueberry, thimbleberry, twinflower and bunchberry with Queen's cup, devil's club, skunk cabbage, deer cabbage, ferns, mosses, lichen and fungi. King or Blue Gentian is found at Blue Gentian Lake in late August and early September, the time of abundant wild blueberries. Red-breasted Sapsuckers and other woodpecker species are present, Blue Grouse and Rufus Hummingbird can be found in cleared areas. Bald Eagles roost on snags and smaller woodland birds such as Bushtits, chickadees and kinglets flit through the canopy. Sunlit brushy edges attract Wilson's, Orange-crowned and MacGillivray's warblers.

Best Time to Visit: May through early summer is best for birdlife and forest floor flowers and sub-alpine flora but the forest trails are accessible year round except during periods of heavy snow.

Bus Service: West Vancouver bus #254 British Properties leaves Downtown Vancouver weekdays during rush hours (7:50 a.m. to 8:25 a.m, and 3:45 p.m. to 5:30 p.m.) or may be transferred to at Park Royal at other times. From Monday to Saturday the service is hourly but on Sundays and holidays there are only three buses during the whole day. Leave the bus at Eyremont Drive and Crestline Road. This is a one way route, clockwise (reversed early weekday mornings), through the British Properties so you should get off and on at the same, or nearby, bus stop for your return. A phone call to West Vancouver Transit Information at 985-7777 should be made to confirm departure times. Bus travel time is 15 minutes from Marine Drive to Eyremount and Crestline Road plus 15 minutes from Downtown Vancouver.

Access: From the bus stop, walk up Crestline Road to Henlow Road (1 block), left on Henlow Rd (1 short block), right on Millstream to 1121 Millstream Road (1 block) where the trailhead is located. Within 250 m the trail crosses the Baden-Powell/Skyline Trail: right to the upper part of Capilano River Regional Park and over Cleveland Dam (3 km and a North Vancouver bus) or left and upward to Ballantree Park (1.5 km), Brothers Creek (2.8 km) or Lost Lake (3.3 km). Beyond and within Cypress Provincial Park connecting trails lead to Blue Gentian Lake, West Lake, First Lake or Fourth Lake. Signposts at junctions give distances and walking times (without stops for naturalizing!) and trails are designated with color coded markers to minimize confusion.

Hazards: Bears frequent these slopes. Attention to direction must be given to avoid getting lost. There is no bus transport to or from Cypress Provincial Park so one must return to the trailhead on Millstream Road.

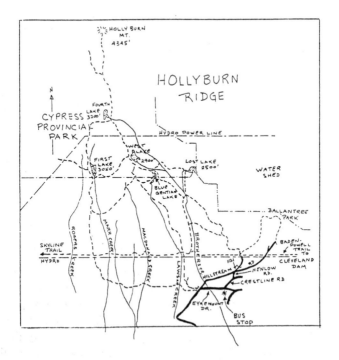

Trails on Hollyburn Ridge

LIGHTHOUSE PARK

For the naturalist, Lighthouse Park offers a marvellous variety within its 75 hectares (188 ac). The lighthouse at Point Atkinson, its first light dating from 1875, was recently designated a National Heritage Site. The diversity of environmental conditions within the park boundaries and the relatively undisturbed forest provide an opportunity to see both Coastal Douglas-fir Zone and Coastal Western Hemlock Zone vegetation in near virgin states. Differences in rainfall and topography create microhabitats producing a wide spectrum of flora and fauna. Headlands and granite outcrops with glacial grooving, surrounded on three sides by the sea, provide a spectacular setting for 400 year old Douglas-fir, a diversity of vegetation types and over 150 bird species.

Giant Douglas-fir dominate the forest, with western redcedar, western hemlock and less common western yew, Sitka spruce and grand fir. Deciduous trees such as red alder and bigleaf maple form the understorey. Dry, rocky bluffs along the shoreline support arbutus trees, false box and, uncommonly, white fawn, chocolate and easter lilies with beach pea and gumweed in areas exposed to ocean spray. In the park's interior, high rocky outcrops rising quickly to 100+m with deep moist valleys encourage a luxuriant vegetation dominated by salmonberry, salal and Oregon grape. Ferns, mosses, skunk cabbage, rushes and sedges inhabit damper or swampy areas. Blue Grouse and Bald Eagle breed in the park while Western Screech Owl, Pileated Woodpecker, Brown Creeper and Hutton's Vireo are found year round. Harlequin Duck and Black Oystercatcher are usually present in the sea or on rocky islets offshore.

Best Time to Visit: Spring and fall migration are most rewarding for birdwatching while wintering waterfowl and resident forest birds promise good all season birding. Wildflowers are best from April to early July.

Bus Service: West Vancouver bus #250 Horseshoe Bay leaves Downtown Vancouver via Georgia Street, crosses Lions Gate Bridge and follows Marine Drive, passing Lighthouse Park. Bus travel time is 35 minutes from Downtown Vancouver.

Access: Ask the bus driver to let you off at Lighthouse Park (sign). Walk south on Beacon Lane 2 blocks to the park entrance and parking lot. A map near the centre of the parking area shows the park with its 5 km of colour coded woodland and shoreline trails. The main trail south leads to the lighthouse and facilities.

Adjacent to Lighthouse Park and flanking it on either side are two smaller parks. Klootchman Park, to the west, gives a good vantage for viewing the Grebe Islets, a unique birding site where Surfbird, Rock Sandpiper and Ruddy Turnstone are often present in fall. From the same bus stop at Beacon Lane walk west along Marine Drive 100 m to Howe Sound Lane, south 100 m just past the junction of The Byway where the trailhead to the seaside begins. To the east of Lighthouse Park is Caulfeild Park, a sandy strip of shoreline and a small cove also good for birdwatching. Ask your driver to let you off at Piccadilly North and look for the access point on the south side of Marine Drive.

Hazards: Precipitous cliffs should be approached with caution and slippery rock faces, trails and steps require sturdy walking footwear with good gripping tread.

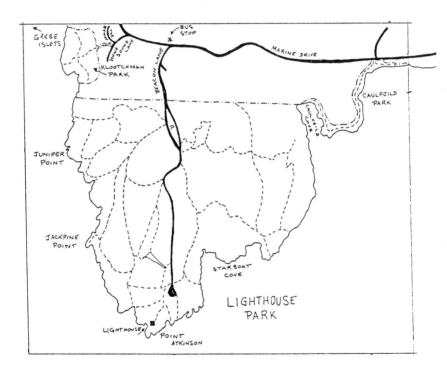

Trails in Lighthouse Park

MOUNT SEYMOUR
PROVINCIAL PARK

Mount Seymour Provincial Park is one of our best known provincial parks. Its forested slopes rise from an elevation of 100 m above sea level to approximately 1,400 m. The park has an extensive network of trails, both on lower slopes and in the sub-alpine.

The slopes of the park above about 1,000 m are in the Mountain Hemlock Zone where yellow cedar, mountain hemlock and amabilis fir are the dominant tree species. Three trails are of special interest to nature enthusiasts:

(1)   Mystery Peak/Mystery Lake Circuit
(2)   Goldie/Flower Lakes circuit
(3)   Dog Mountain Trail

A favourite is the approximately 3 km Goldie/Flower Lakes loop, where you can enjoy the trees, birds and wildflowers that characterize a sub-alpine forest. Part of Goldie Lake is a marsh with interesting plants such as fringed grass-of-parnassus, leather-leaf mountain daisy and Sitka mountain ash. Birds include the Gray Jay ("Whisky Jack"), Common Raven and Northern Pygmy-Owl (the park is a favourite place to see this species).

In summer, you can also observe the northwestern (brown) salamander in the shallows to the lakes. Nibbled fireweed plants are a sure sign that black-tailed deer are in the area.

The main trail of the park's lower slopes is the 37 km Baden-Powell Trail which extends from Horseshoe Bay to Deep Cove along the North Shore mountains.

Mount Seymour Road is intersected by the trail about 2 km up from the park entrance. The trail continues to Indian River Road and goes left along the road a short distance, to the hydro right-of-way, or the slightly longer route just past the power lines that leads to a lookout over Indian Arm. From here the trail comes up under the power lines to join the short route and carry on down to Deep Cove.

A 3 - 3.5 km walk taking 1.5 - 2 hrs begins at the #211 Seymour or #212 Dollarton bus stop at the end of Gallant. The eastern terminus of the trail is located a short distance north from Gallant on Panorama Drive in Deep Cove.
The walk through this mixed (second growth) forest is quite lovely, especially in

late spring/early summer. Trees consist of western hemlock, western redcedar, Douglas-fir, bigleaf maple and red alder.

The forest floor and nurse logs are decorated with a beautiful carpet of mosses and liverworts. Six species of ferns are common here including spiny wood, western shield, western sword, deer and lady ferns, with licorice fern growing off the forest floor on the sides of maples.

Birding is best in spring when Black-throated Gray Warbler, Warbling Vireo, and Orange-crowned Warbler return from their South American wintering grounds. The beautiful song of the Winter Wren is usually heard somewhere along the trail. It is also a good place to see Pileated and Hairy Woodpecker and Red-breasted Sapsucker.

Each season has its own rewards along this trail, which is a pleasant introduction to a second growth west coast hemlock forest.

Bus Service: The main bus loop in this area, Phibbs Exchange, is at the north end of the Second Narrows bridge. From here you will get a #211 Seymour bus which goes along Mount Seymour Parkway. Get off at the Parkgate Shopping Centre and walk north. Soon you will come to a large carved portal sign and small grassy picnic site. On the notice board is a map of the park, showing trails. The Vancouver District Office of BC Parks is located to the right of the park gate, where you can get a map of the park and a Bird Checklist.

Access: Many people hike or cycle up the 8 km road to the Upper Parking Lot at 1,000 m elevation. If you don't have a car, it is suggested that a group of 3 or 4 go together and share the taxi fare, thus making it quite economical.

Douglas Squirrel

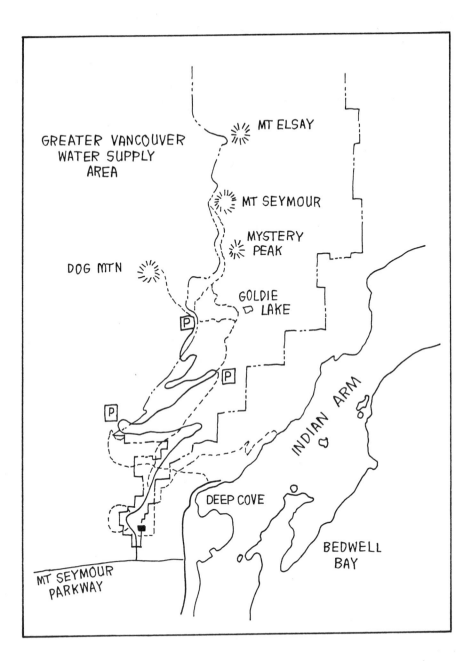

Mount Seymour Provincial Park

Raccoon

MAPLE RIDGE

Golden-crowned Kinglet

Trillium

KANAKA CREEK

Kanaka Creek Regional Park preserves a natural stream corridor, with second growth forests, meadows, and marshes. Natural highlights of the park include the two waterfalls over sandstone cliffs at the Cliff Falls area. In addition to providing many wildlife habitats, Kanaka Creek is interesting geologically. Interbedded sandstone and shale of Tertiary age (Eocene to Oligocene, between 58 and 24 million years ago) contain remains of ancient forests. Leaf and fern fossils can be seen in silty layers eroded by the creek, along with fossil tree trunks and minor coal seams. These plant fossils indicate a relatively warmer, more tropical climate during the Eocene than we have here in Vancouver today. The headwaters of Kanaka Creek start in Jurassic quartz diorite. The creek then flows through Pleistocene glacial deposits before cutting down through the Tertiary sandstone featured in the waterfalls, and at the confluence of Kanaka Creek and the Fraser River, younger glacial drift and delta sediments underlie the two streams.

Some of the natural inhabitants are salmon, trout, herons, woodpeckers, and rare tailed frogs. The fish hatchery is an interesting place to visit, and has a staffed visitor centre.

A horseback riding trail goes through the north side of the park. Hiking trails are relatively easy and go through second growth forest. The dominant trees above the creek are bigleaf maple. From the forest core area (toward Blue Mountain) at the headwaters of Kanaka Creek, through the woodsy reaches above the waterfalls, to the marshy delta area at the Fraser Riverfront, Kanaka Creek offers a diversity of bird-watching areas as well.

Bus Service: Kanaka Creek Regional Park is a GVRD park located in Maple Ridge, accessible by public transit from Dewdney Trunk Road at Webster's Corner (256 Street). It comprises a 12 km-long narrow area of about 400 ha along Kanaka Creek from where it joins the Fraser River at Lougheed Highway.

Access: The part of Kanaka Creek Park most visited is a section accessible from either 252 Street or 256 Street and Dewdney Trunk Road; it would be about a 1 km walk to the south on either street. The route on 256 Street leads to the Bell-Irving Kanaka Creek Fish Hatchery, and the route on 252 (and 251 Street) leads to the Cliff Falls area, about 1.5 km west of the Fish Hatchery. There are outhouses at both ends of this section of the park.

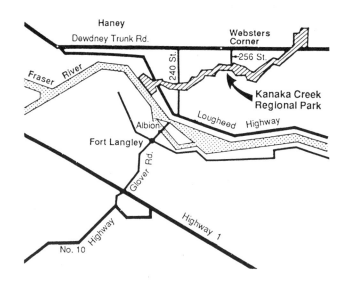

Location of Kanaka Creek Regional Park

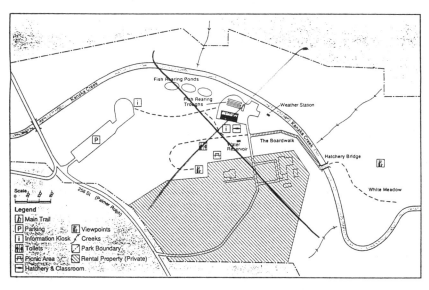

Bell-Irving Fish Hatchery

Wandering Tattler

Common Goldeneye

PORT MOODY SHORELINE PARK

Port Moody Arm forms the crescent shaped easternmost tip of Burrard Inlet. The Shoreline Trail runs for 3 km from the head of Port Moody Arm at Rocky Point Park to the opposite shore at Old Orchard Park. For most of its length the trail hugs the shore providing excellent views of the foreshore, the mudflats and the open water. About 120 bird species were identified in this area during a study conducted by the Burke Mountain Naturalists and the Burrard Inlet Environmental Action Program during 1993-94. The shoreline and mudflats are best for birding, especially at dawn and dusk.

The Noons Creek watershed cuts the Shoreline Park in half. There is a salmon and trout teaching hatchery about 200 m upstream from the shoreline trail. Visitors are welcome. A survey of nesting birds in the Noons Creek Watershed was conducted in 1993-94 by the Douglas College Institute of Urban Ecology, Port Moody Ecological Society and the Friends of the Environment Foundation.

A new species of nematode (small round worm) was recently discovered at the Old Mill site. The Mudflats contain an abundance of intertidal marine life, best seen at low tide (wear rubber boots). There are also many salt marsh plants.

The walking trail is paralleled by a paved bike path from end to end.

Access: The Shoreline Trail can be reached from several points: Rocky Point Park, Old Orchard Beach, the Port Moody recreation centre, Pigeon Cove and the Railway crossing. There are also any number of smaller trails in the area leading to the park.

Bus Service: Port Moody Shoreline Park can be reached by the # 148 IOCO bus from Lougheed Mall and Coquitlam Centre.

Best Time to Visit: Dawn or dusk and at low tides. Fall and Spring migrations are especially good for birds.

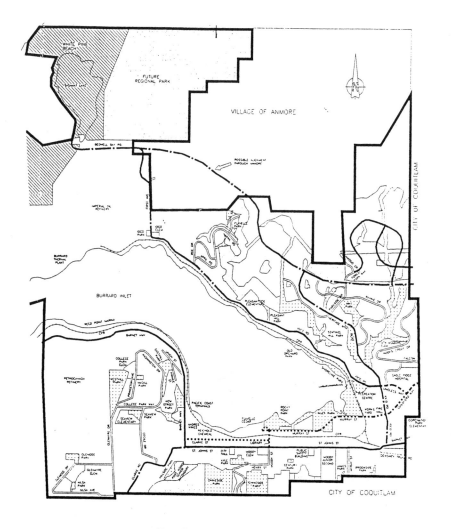

Port Moody Shoreline Park

Red Tailed
~~**Rough-legged**~~ *Hawk*

Grand Fir

RICHMOND NATURE PARK

The heart of Lulu Island is the site of the Richmond Nature Park, established as a park in the early 70's to preserve a sample of raised bog and bog forest. This is one of few natural areas left in the interior of the Island.

Typical plants of the bog include sphagnum mosses, Labrador tea, cranberry, blueberries, bog laurel and shore pine. Winding trails throughout the bog give visitors a sense that the park is much bigger than its 45 ha (112 ac).

The Richmond Nature Park is open daily dawn to dusk. The Nature House is open daily 9:00 am - 5:00 pm and admission is free. Visit the Nature House to view exhibits about the bog, a small live animal display, use the library or browse in the gift shop. While in the Nature House pick up a trail guide or information on public programs. The Nature House is fully accessible to wheelchairs.

Best Time to Visit:

Spring: The bog blooms in spring - clusters of creamy Labrador tea, bog laurel and cranberry. Spring birds include warblers and hummingbirds.

Summer: Carnivorous sundew plants may be seen. The pond is a good place to view dragonfly behaviour in July and August.

Fall: Excellent fall colour as the blueberries prepare for winter. Large numbers of migrating American Robin and Cedar Waxwing feed on late berries.

Winter: A good viewing place for Rufous-sided Towhee, Black-capped Chickadee, Winter Wren and Dark-eyed Junco.

Bus Service: #405 Five Road along Westminster Highway from Richmond Centre.

Access: The address of the Richmond Nature Park is 11851 Westminster Hwy, Richmond, BC V6X 1B4. Enter the Park at the well marked sign on Westminster Highway just west of No.5 Road.

All the trails start and return to the Nature House. Trails are level bark mulch and well marked. Trails may be a bit "boggy" in winter wet spells.

Hazards: Visitors are cautioned to remain on trails to avoid getting lost in the shrubbery of the bog.

Bog Laurel

STEVESTON

The community of Steveston is situated in Richmond, at the southwestern tip of Lulu Island. It has been an important fishing port for over a century, and the Gulf of Georgia Cannery, now preserved as a national historic site, is well worth a visit. A public fish sales float is also located here. The actual southwestern extremity, Garry Point, is a popular public park offering views across the Strait of Georgia to the Gulf Islands, over the Fraser River to Reifel Island, and eastwards into Cannery Channel, where many fish boats find moorage.

The dyke above Sturgeon Bank runs northwards from Garry Point, and is well-used by walkers and cyclists, as well as being popular with birders. Although still rich in bird life, the populations are less than previously, as most of the adjacent farmland has been built upon. During the growing season the estuarine marshlands are a beautiful sight. The plants here grow in distinct zones. Where different species occur depends upon the amount of brackish water tidal inundation they can tolerate. Unfortunately the plant most admired by the average visitor is the invading purple loosestrife, a serious noxious weed.

Bus Service: #406 Railway (From Burrard Station at Burrard and Dunsmuir Streets, eventually travels along Howe Street and Granville Street to Richmond). Get off at 7th Avenue and Chatham Street in Steveston at the southwestern tip of Richmond. Another possibility is #407, which goes as far as 4th and Chatham. Bus travel time is one hour from Burrard Station.

Access: For Garry Point Park walk westwards from 7th Avenue and Chatham Street, into the adjacent park. The dyke parallel to Sturgeon Bank may be followed northwards from near the entrance of the park. To visit the Gulf of Georgia Cannery proceed east on Chatham Street to 4th Avenue and south on 4th for about a block to the cannery.

Best Time to Visit: Marsh plants at their best from July to October. Many Snow Geese, as well as raptors and waterfowl in winter. Songbirds can be seen from spring to fall.

Hazards: The dyke path is very popular on weekends, and is extensively used by cyclists. Do not venture onto the marshlands themselves because of the danger of sinking, and also because of the accompanying environmental damage.

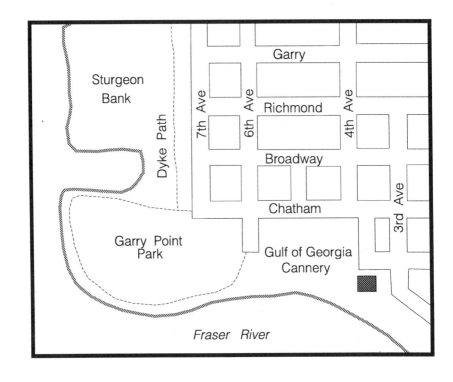

Steveston

Looking at marine life

DELTA

Bog Cranberry

Dragonfly

BURNS BOG

Ten thousand years ago the Lower Mainland was under 5,000 feet of ice. As the ice receded the Fraser Delta was formed, and Burns Bog became a peat bog, about 3,500 years ago. Burns Bog is now the largest urban green space in Greater Vancouver. The bog is 4,000 ha (10,000 ac) in area, about 10 times the size of Stanley Park. It was named after Dominic Burns of Burns Meats, who at one time owned the bog and grazed cattle there.

Bogs form in areas of little or no drainage. They rely on rain as their primary source of water, and do not have any significant outflows from streams. As a result of this, the acids released from decaying organic matter accumulate, creating a unique acidic ecosystem. A bog is characterized by sphagnum moss, the material which makes peat when it dies. Sphagnum moss not only tolerates acidity but also promotes it to reduce competition from other plants.

In addition to withstanding acidity, bog plants show adaptations to prevent water loss (the acidic water is largely unusable by the plants, who are living in a "liquid desert"). Labrador tea (yes, the dried leaves do make a nice tea), has red furry undersides of curled leaves to trap in moisture. Bog cranberry and swamp laurel have thick waxy cuticles on their leaves, making them tough and shiny, and resistant to water loss.

Bogs are nutrient poor environments as the acidity prevents decomposition of dead plants and release of their nutrients. Some plants have become insectivorous to obtain nutrients from insects instead of the soil. The sundew plant, which traps insects on its sticky leaves, is common in bogs and is a treat to discover.

Some plants in Burns Bog are considered remnants of the last ice age. Cloudberry, crowberry and velvet-leaved blueberry were left behind as the glaciers receded and are all at the southern-most limit of their distribution.

A common tree growing in the higher elevations of the bog is the shore pine. This tree is called the lodgepole pine in the interior, where it grows straight and tall and is good for making cabins. In the harsh bog environment, on the other hand, the tree is stunted by the lack of nutrients, hence its scientific name *Pinus contorta*.

Burns Bog is next to the Fraser estuary and is used by many birds migrating along the Pacific Flyway. Over 150 species of birds can be seen here, and 28 species of mammals, including black bear, bobcat, blacktailed deer, porcupine and beaver.

Most of Burns Bog is privately owned and not accessible to the public. About 10% of the southwest corner is the Vancouver Landfill, used to dispose of more than half of the region's garbage annually.

Access: About 5% of Burns Bog is in the Delta Nature Reserve and open to the public. The trail through the Delta Nature Reserve begins at the junction of 108 St and Monroe Drive. The Burns Bog Conservation Society, formed in 1988, has been active in constructing a boardwalk along much of the trail.

Bus Service: The #312 Scottsdale Mall from the SkyTrain station goes down 112 St. Get off at Monroe Drive and walk down to the trail.

Hazards: The bog can be muddy and wet after a rain. There is also a drainage ditch on the site which can be a hazard.

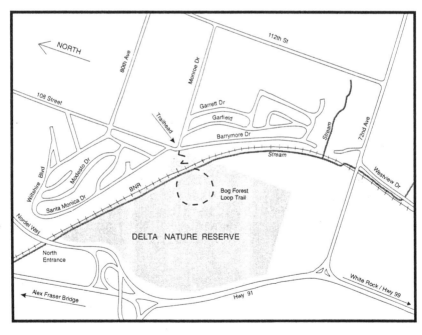

Location of Delta Nature Reserve,
Burns Bog

Sea Asparagus (Salicornia)

Wood Ducks

BLACKIE SPIT

Blackie Spit is a well known destination for Vancouver birders. It provides access to the south side of Mud Bay and is one of the better places in the lower mainland to see some of the larger locally rare shorebirds such as Willet, Marbled Godwit and Long-billed Curlew. In recent years one of each of these species and a whimbrel have spent the winter at the spit and are called the "amigos" by local birders. Blackie Spit can also be a good place to see gulls, ducks and many of the more common shorebirds of the Vancouver area.

The areas of interest include the spit itself (Lapland Longspur and Snow Bunting possible in the appropriate seasons), the waters of Mud Bay (loons, grebes and waterfowl), the shallow waters and salt marsh on the eastern side of the spit (ducks, gulls and shorebirds), the tidal pond and Farm Slough yet farther east (ducks and shorebirds; sparrows and finches in small trees around tidal pond in winter). It can also be productive to follow the trail under the railroad tracks and check out the lower reaches of the Nicomekl River (a rare Yellow-billed Loon was seen here in January, 1994).

The vegetation at Blackie Spit consists of various grasses, shrubs and small trees. The saltmarsh areas have other plants of interest such as glasswort.

Best time to visit: The level of the tide is very important for reasonable viewing of the birds. At low tide, a huge area of mudflats is exposed and the birds can be too distant to identify. During a very high tide (4.5 m or more) the birds are forced to go elsewhere as their roosting areas are submerged. Optimal tides for shorebirds are 3.0 to 3.8 m; plan to arrive at least one hour before the expected optimal viewing time. Rising tides are the best time to view shorebirds; check your local newspaper for times. Apart from tide considerations, Blackie Spit can provide a rewarding outing at any time of year with the greatest variety of shorebirds present in summer and fall.

Bus Service: Blackie Spit is easily reached by public transit although a fair commitment of time is required (almost 1.5 hours each way from downtown Vancouver). A visit to Blackie Spit can be combined with a visit to the White Rock waterfront as the bus goes through White Rock before reaching Blackie Spit. The #351 Cresent Beach bus starts at the Burrard Skytrain Station, and eventually travels along the King George Hwy into White Rock. It then continues west through White Rock and north to Crescent Beach. The stop you want is the next to last one at the corner of Sullivan and McBride. From the stop it is a short walk down McBride (10 minutes) through a large parking lot (toilets available) to the base of the spit. Service is hourly (half-hourly weekdays). Return is by the same route in reverse.

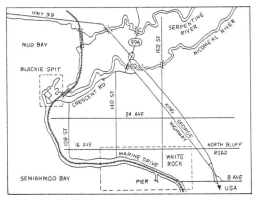

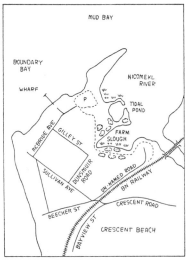

South Surrey and Blackie Spit

BOUNDARY BAY

Boundary Bay is an exciting, biologically diverse area, where many aspects of nature may be enjoyed, both birds and plants. Highlights include:

- raptors - a nationally significant wintering area
- owls - Barn, Snowy (numbers vary from year to year), Short-eared, Long-eared, and Great Horned are found here
- interesting salt marsh plant communities
- locally rare butterflies
- internationally significant migrating/wintering shorebird habitat
- wintering/migrating area for Brant (a sea goose) and other waterfowl

Bus Service: Whichever way you come, you will need to get to Ladner Ring near the highway 10 and 17 junction. From here you can catch the following buses:

#601 Boundary Bay (from South Delta Recreation Centre); #603 Beach Grove (from South Delta Recreation Centre; in the am and pm rush hours also from and to Vancouver); or #640 from Scott Road/Surrey Central Stations. It is vital to check an up-to-date schedule.

Access: Boundary Bay is a vast area, not all of it readily accessible by transit. However, if you are prepared to do some easy walking, the best nature viewing spots are yours to enjoy.

Two access points convenient by transit are:

(1)   Delta Airport area (72nd)
(2)   Tsawwassen Area at the foot of 12th with access to Beach Grove.

PLAN A

Get off at the foot of 12th in Tsawwassen. This will give you access to a wonderful tidal lagoon. Straight ahead there is an excellent place to observe migrating shorebirds including Western Sandpiper, Semi-palmated Plover and Greater and Lesser Yellowleg. Wintering ducks include Green-winged Teal, Northern Pintail and American Wigeon.

Nearby blackberry tangles are good havens for sparrows including Golden and

White-crowned, with a good chance of spotting a rarer Lincoln's or Harris' Sparrow.

Walk ahead along the dyke and soon the path curves to the right. The bend is a good place to look for wintering and migrating Brant. Continuing along the dyke, on your right is Boundary Bay Regional Park; the far end (south) is known as Centennial Park. This is a fascinating "sand dune" community complete with field crickets, tiger beetles and plants that show adaptations for a dry environment such as the Indian consumption plant, one of the larval foods of the locally scarce anise swallowtail butterfly. Some wildflowers of this area include blue-eyed Mary and vernal whitlow grass. The fields and surrounding trees and shrubs attract various raptors such as Northern Harrier, Red-tailed and Rough-legged Hawks. It is one of the better places in the Lower Mainland to watch for falcons such as the Merlin or Peregrine.

Another interesting trip is to take the Beach Grove bus, getting off at Beach Grove Park (beside a school). From here there is a path (to the right of the small woodlot facing east) that will get you down to the dyke that skirts Boundary Bay.

Before you head round the bay, spend some time at Beach Grove Park. Tall cottonwoods here always attract Bald Eagles as well as other raptors. In denser trees (mostly hawthorn) you may be able to spot a Great Horned or Long-eared Owl (this has been one of the more reliable sites to see them). Tangles of small bushes are usually full of small birds such as sparrows and Bewick's Wrens.

Many of the coniferous trees are grand fir, a true fir whose cones stand upright (unlike a Douglas-fir whose cones hang down).

At the back of the dyke, bear to the left (north) where before you lies Boundary Bay, the foreshore area and agricultural fields. This area has been called one of the most biologically significant in North America. Migrating shorebirds from the high north pass through here. Some, such as Dunlin, pause on their way to wintering grounds in South America. Thus, there is a direct linkage between breeding grounds, feeding/migratory sites and wintering area.

Scanning over the foreshore, check out the following:

·   Shorebirds - large flocks that "flash" dark to light, moving in sinuous clouds are Dunlin.

·   Raptors - hawks and eagles including the Rough-legged Hawk. Merlins are often seen in winter, hunting Dunlin over the foreshore.

· Owls - both Short-eared Owls (which breed here) and Snowy Owls (win ter) are seen here, with numbers varying from year to year.

· Plants - interesting salt marsh plant communities consisting of plants adapted to growing in intertidal saline marshes. They include the sea asparagus of culinary fame, also known as salt water pickle or glasswort. In summer, a stringy plant parasitic on sea asparagus known as dodder forms bright orange mats in the marsh. The rare pale montia also grows on the sand flats just north of Centennial Beach.

· Mammals - spread apart low grass and you will discover runways of voles, small rodents that are the main food source of many predatory birds. Coyotes are regularly seen along this dyke, hunting the voles.

You can continue along the dyke for several more kilometres until you reach 64th, then it is a good 1 1/2 hour walk to Hwy 10. This makes a nice day, especially if you are interested in hawk watching. Or, you can return to Beach Grove, and back to Delta Recreation Centre and Ladner Ring or Vancouver.

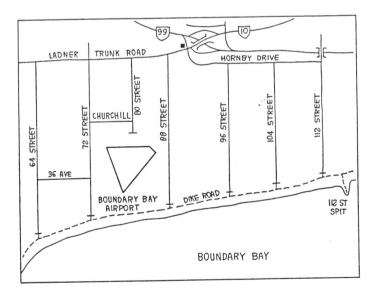

Boundary Bay access points

PLAN B

Start from Ladner Ring and catch a #640 Scott Road/Surrey Central Station. Get off at 72nd St. and Highway 10. If you walk north you will come to a large culvert under the freeway that you can walk through to the fields near the Vancouver Landfill. In winter, nearby fields often have swans (mainly Trumpeter and possibly Tundra). Surrounding tree and shrubs are always good for raptors.

By walking south along 72nd St., you follow a hedgerow of small trees. Check it for possible owls (Long-eared, Saw-whet) and various sparrows.

Once you have crossed the tracks can you see the airport, where there is a very nice coffee shop. You can walk round the edge of the airport, because it is always excellent for raptors, *BUT DO NOT TRESPASS.* Along the west side of the airport, parallel to the road, is a hedge of one-seeded hawthorn. This imported species is the most commonly encountered hawthorn in the area, although there is a native black fruited hawthorn. Hawthorn fruits attract birds such American Robin and Cedar Waxwing, especially in late winter when other fruits are scarce.

Wood Duck

You can continue walking south on 72nd St. to the dyke, where you can walk (south) to the right, finally winding up at Beach Grove, an all day hike.

It is also feasible to take the #640 and get off at Matthews Exchange, near where highways 10 and 99 meet. This will allow you to walk along 88th St., also winding up at the Boundary Bay Dyke where you can walk eastward to 112th St., a place that always produces interesting birds. In summer, yellow daisy-like flowers of gumweed add their colour to the landscape, which are present till fall when Douglas asters bloom.

Walk back to 112th St. and Highway 10 for the ride back to Ladner Ring or Surrey Central Station (access to SkyTrain).

To do Boundary Bay comfortably, you will need an entire day and good weather. Be prepared to do some walking (at least 7 - 10 km). Bring a lunch and something to drink. Please bring a bus schedule and watch the time!

Boundary Bay has been recognized for its special biological importance. In the next few years, there will no doubt be many changes - some good, some doubtful. It is yours to enjoy and to cherish.

Bald Eagle

Western Kingbird

BIRDING FROM SKYTRAIN

The changing scene along the almost 22 km length of the SkyTrain's route is fascinating. Reading the landscape is a most enjoyable way to ride the SkyTrain. One can study land use patterns, topography, trees, and birds.

Along its length from New Westminster to the Vancouver waterfront, the SkyTrain passes through a wide variety of suburban and urban landscapes. Even so the route is well treed, mostly with imported species such as Lombardy poplar and cherry. After leaving New Westminster Station, you can see the cottonwoods along the Fraser River as well as Bald Eagle and Red-tailed Hawk. Most waterfowl on the river are too distant to identify, but Mallard and Canada Geese can be seen.

From 22nd Steet Station to Burnaby's Metrotown, the landscape varies from groves of alders to young cottonwoods and typical suburban gardens. Near Edmonds Station, the SkyTrain passes near Ron McLean Park, a wooded area of mixed deciduous-coniferous trees. Typically, House Finch, Evening Grosbeak and Pine Siskin may be seen flitting between the trees.

By the time the SkyTrain reaches the Royal Oak - Metrotown area there is little natural vegetation except for a grove of Douglas-firs at Bonsor Park. In this stretch of the line Crested Myna are regularly seen. Predictably, "citified" species such as the House Sparrow, European Starling, and Northwestern Crow are abundant here. This may relate to the refuse that is generated by the large shopping centre.

Between Metrotown and Joyce Station is Central Park, a large area of coniferous forest and playing fields. Occasionally an accipiter is spotted, and finches, with their typical "dancing" flight, are also seen. The park fields are often grazed by up to 100 Canada Geese at a time. Mallard frequently fly in and out of the woods since the park has several small lakes. Band-tailed Pigeon can be spotted in the trees.

Past Joyce Station there are glorious views of the North Shore Mountains - marvellous on a cold, clear winter day! Looking down onto Trout Lake in John Hendry Park, one can spot wigeon, Mallard, scaup, and Bufflehead. Also, the occasional Merlin or Sharp-shinned Hawk flashes past.

Near Broadway Station, the track follows a deep ravine where freight and passenger trains pass. This gully is well treed and some House Finch, starlings, and crows reside here.

Soon the industrial area between Broadway Station and Science World - Main Street Station is at hand, with its freight and railroad marshalling yards. It hardly seems to be good bird habitat, but there are many forgotten corners and weedy patches.

Just past Main Street Station, False Creek is the first major water habitat we encounter, with Western Grebes, Canada Geese, and a variety of ducks. It is often possible to see a Great Blue Heron in the distance along False Creek.

The section from Burrard Station to the Waterfront Station is largely barren of birds. The usual House Sparrow and European Starling are there, and there are Glaucous-winged Gull on the rooftops - just sitting and perhaps even nesting.

The SkyTrain terminates at the Burrard Inlet waterfront. The SeaBus voyage across Burrard Inlet takes the traveller to Lonsdale Quay in North Vancouver. Burrard Inlet is a major marine habitat and gulls, grebes, ducks and alcids may be seen during the 15 minute crossing.

The months from mid-November to early March offer the best birding from the SkyTrain and the SeaBus.

Black-capped chickadee

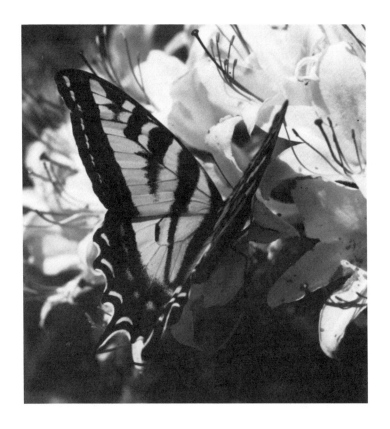

Western *Tiger Swallowtail*

Exploring an Ant Nest

GALIANO ISLAND
BELLHOUSE PROVINCIAL PARK AND BLUFF PARK

Galiano Island is a perfect one day bus/boating nature adventure. Galiano Island, one of the Gulf Islands, must surely be one of Canada's loveliest places, with its combination of sun, land and sea. Here is a wonderful place to go "naturing" where every season has its own special discoveries, whether it be the geology, birds, mammals or what has been called its "California-like" flora. Add to this the fact that the people of Galiano are very special - fiercely proud of their island.

Bus Service: Getting to Galiano Island by transit is easy, in fact, its the perfect way to go. It is very important, however, to equip yourself with both BC Transit and BC Ferry schedules and to appreciate that changes can be regularly made.

Whatever route you take, you will need to get to Ladner Ring (the major South Delta bus loop). From there you will take the bus to the BC Ferry Terminal at Tsawwassen. This is the plan, no matter what direction you are coming from. The Saturday morning ferry (the best day if weekends are your only option) leaves at 9:25 am.

At the ferry terminal you may have time to have a snack in the cafeteria and spend a bit of time looking among the rocks of the causeway for Black Oystercatcher and Black Turnstone; or offshore at the ducks, loons, grebes and cormorants. The ferry terminal area is actually quite a fine birding spot. In spring you will be treated to Brant feeding there, on their way north to their breeding grounds.

ON THE FERRY

If you have caught the 9:25 am sailing, you should arrive at Sturdies Bay, the first port-of-call, and where you get off, about 10:15 - 10:30. Listen carefully for the announcement on the PA, otherwise you will wind up at Mayne Island. To make a good day of it, you will want to catch the 5:50 pm sailing back to Tsawwassen (check the ferry schedule - otherwise you may have to stay overnight).

In fact, there are fine Bed and Breakfasts on the island, and many of the owners will come and get you at the ferry. The Islanders produce a nice brochure which gives a bit of the Island's history, has a map and lists the Bed and Breakfasts; one offers a marine nature trip aboard a sailboat. Brochures can be picked up from the ferry's brochure rack.

On board the ferry, you will want to grab a quick breakfast, because you should be out on deck watching for birds and mammals. This is especially true as you pass by Fairway Bank, on the approach to Active Pass, which separates Galiano from Mayne Island. Depending on the season, this is a gathering place for hundreds (even thousands) of Pacific Loon, Bonaparte's Gull, Mew Gull and Brandt's Cormorant. In fall Parasitic Jaegers may often be seen chasing Common Tern, whose regurgitated meals of fish are quickly snapped up by their pursuers. Watch also for (in smaller numbers) Pigeon Guillemot, Marbled Murrelet and Common Murre, all belonging to a group of birds called alcids. These are said to take the place of penguins in the Northern Hemisphere.

With any luck you may also be able to spot killer whales *(orcas)*, porpoises or seals.

ON THE ISLAND

Now that you are on the island, it should be pointed out that washrooms are scarce. At the time of writing there are public washrooms at Sturdies Bay ferry terminal and pit toilets at Bellhouse Provincial Park. There are washrooms in coffee shops, should you decide to have a snack or lunch.

From Sturdies Bay, it is 1 km to Bellhouse Provincial Park - just follow the signs. En route, you will pass by the picturesque Whaler Bay, a name that gives a hint of past activity on the island. You might also want to stop at the roadside Information Centre to pick up a small map if you have not got one already. The route is a pleasant stroll, past the old church of St. Margaret of Scotland.

Keep your eyes on the roadsides for wildflowers - it is a very good island for roadside flora where you can find good patches of cranesbill and dove's foot geranium. Honeysuckle twines around fences and hedges.

AT BELLHOUSE

Despite its small size the park has an amazing diversity of plant life. It is also listed as a wildlife viewing site with eagles, sea lions, killer whales and a variety of sea birds possible.

Galiano Island is located in the Strait of Georgia and the park is part of the Georgian Depression Ecoprovince. Within this landscape are fine examples of large arbutus scattered amongst stately Douglas-fir and grand fir. On open sites, stunted "wind sculptured" Garry oaks show their tenacity.

Chocolate lily, western buttercup and snake-root carpet the ground while orange and red honeysuckle wrap themselves around trees and shrubs providing nectar for hummingbirds. Open bluffs are populated with red maids, broad-leafed stonecrop and tomcat clover. Yellow monkey flowers secure themselves near water seepage and put on a showy display. Each April white fawn lily (Easter lily) puts on an excellent show at the park's west end. .

Bellhouse Park, a gift to the Province of British Columbia from the Bellhouse family, is a pleasure to visit during any season each offering something different. As well, it's a park where you can leave your car at the ferry dock and walk the 1 km from the ferry terminal at Sturdies Bay, along a pleasant country road.

Bellhouse is a good place to have your packed lunch. You will also want to explore the shoreline to admire the sculpted sandstone, which offers some wonderful photographic opportunities. Best time to visit the park so that you get a good combination of birds and flowers is mid-April.

OFF TO BLUFF PARK

About 1 1/2 hour stroll from Bellhouse is Bluff Park. You go back along the road that leads into the park; where it joins the main road (Burrill Road) turn left (south) and continue along past a fine view of Active Pass and Mayne Island, up a slight grade, past some pasture (look along the edge here for blacktail deer). Soon the road begins to climb until you see a sign at the park gate - Bluff Park. Walk straight ahead for 15 minutes or so until you see the sign that tells you this is a community park, run by citizens of the island. Please pack out ALL YOUR GARBAGE - this should be a rule for the whole island. If you see litter, pick it up, even if it is not yours. Turn left at the sign and within minutes you will be treated to one of the grandest views anywhere. Before you stretch the Gulf Islands, including Mayne, Prevost and Saltspring. Below you is Active Pass, with its busy marine traffic.

Two things (beside the view) make this park outstanding:

(a)   wildflowers, including red maids, spring gold, blue-eyed mary and early saxifrage - these are on the grassy bluffs

(b)   in the woods you can find spotted coral root orchid, calypso orchid and sandwort

There are some lovely trees including lichen festooned Garry oaks.

Birding can also be rewarding. There are usually Bald Eagle and Turkey Vulture, especially in spring and fall. Songbirds include Chestnut-backed Chickadee, Bushtit, House Wren, Bewick's Wren and in summer, Townsend's Warbler and Rufous Hummingbird. There is a small, but marked raptor migration in fall, with Sharp Shinned Hawk and Red-tailed Hawk being the most commonly observed.

An interesting feature of Bluff Park is the difference in plant communities from the north to the south side. The north side has a cedar/swordfern forest, indicating an abundance of moisture; on the south side, Garry oak and arbutus are common, and in some places, prickly pear cactus grows, indicating a drier regime.

From Bluff Park, you can either go back the way that you came (watch your time - you need about 1 1/2 to 2 hours) or you can go to the west (left of the Bluff Park sign down the hill, to Georgeson Bay Road, then follow it back until you come to the Mayne Village/Fire hall, pub, etc.)

Remember the ferry sails at 5:50 - get there a little early. You can always watch cormorants, seals or even otters in Sturdies Bay.

Finally, get yourself a copy of *The Gulf Island Explorer* or another good Gulf Islands guide. The latter has lots of information about the history, natural history and other interesting features of these beautiful islands.

Location of Bellhouse Park and Bluff Park
Galiano Island

NEWCASTLE ISLAND

Newcastle Island is Nanaimo's answer to Stanley Park only there is no vehicle access other than a passenger ferry. The whole island (306 ha or 756 ac), is a provincial marine park. Newcastle boasts an incredibly rich human history. As one of our Gulf Islands its climate is among the mildest in Canada and its vegetation reflects the rainshadow character of south eastern Vancouver Island.

In years past (1931 until the early 1950's) Newcastle was a well known destination for Vancouver residents. The Canadian Pacific Steamship Company purchased the Island in 1931 as a resort recreation destination. Company picnics and family oriented recreation activities were promoted through the construction of a dance pavilion and restaurant. Picnic facilities and recreation opportunities that included ball fields, walking trails, and swimming facilities were also provided.

Today the island is primarily a playground for Nanaimo residents and the yachting enthusiasts who find the island a good place to anchor either as a primary destination or as a stop over during more extended trips.

Facilities on Newcastle include a concession in the pavilion for hot drinks and "fast" food items and public washrooms. Newcastle Island is a warm friendly destination. Interpretive displays in the pavilion and at sites around the island explain much of the islands earlier history. Coal mining, sandstone and pulpstone quarrying, Japanese herring salteries, even the burial site of an axe murderer are among the subjects covered. More than 20 km of wide easily negotiated trails circle and cris cross the island.

For naturalists, Mallard Lake is an easy destination. Originally created to establish a permanent water source for steam production during the island coal mining period, this lake is now frequented by muskrats, beavers and a variety of duck species. Pumpkinseed sunfish are food for Great Blue Heron and Hooded Merganser. Bald Eagle are permanent residents with one or two nesting pairs.

Newcastle is a good bird watching destination. In late spring and early summer Black-throated Grey warbler breed on the island along with the "regular" assortment of forest birds. From the coastal paths and viewpoints Black Oystercatcher, Double-crested and Pelagic Cormorant are frequently seen. Northern Flicker and a few pairs of Pileated Woodpecker are present at all times, but not as easily seen.

Below Giovando lookout, harbour seals regularly use the rocks as haulouts. Both northern and California frequent this area and are seen on a daily basis from November through April.

Newcastle Island is not noted for its great show of spring wildflowers but along open rocky portions of its coastline some very beautiful "gardens" of mimulus, seablush, broad-leaved stone crop, camas and woodland stars occur under a loose canopy of Garry oak and arbutus. Forest trails have good showing of ground cone, evergreen huckleberry, spotted coralroot and starflower. Redmaids can be found in the scuffed up gravel near the top of the landing wharf in May.

Infamous to Newcastle are its "champagne" coloured raccoons. A portion of this population have a genetic condition that does not allow the formation of black pigment in their body hair. As a result these "blonde" individuals are quite a novelty.

Harbour Seal

Barnacles

Visitors to Newcastle should pick up information about the island and its trail system from the ferry operator. Toilets are located at various points along the island's trail system but other than in the dock, campground and pavilion area drinking water is not available. A thermos or canteen is recommended.

Access: From Vancouver there are a number of ways to bus to Newcastle. Direct buses from downtown Vancouver to downtown Nanaimo connect with the regular BC Ferry sailings from Horseshoe Bay (check the current bus and ferry schedules for times). Public transit, the West Vancouver "Blue Buses" depart regularly from Granville and Georgia to Horseshoe Bay. A short walk will take you to the BC Ferry terminal. Once in Nanaimo there is a public bus to the downtown area or there is a waterfront walk (about 2 and 1/2 km) along Newcastle Channel. Whichever bus is taken a short walk will be required to get to the Newcastle Island Ferry dock in Maffeo-Sutton Park beside the Civic arena and just across the highway from the Tally Ho Hotel.

The Newcastle Island Ferry operates daily from the Victoria Day weekend until Thanksgiving weekend and intermittently on weekends, weather permitting. There is a charge for this service ($4.25 return in 1996).

BIBLIOGRAPHY

Armstrong, John E. 1990. *Vancouver Geology.* Edited by Charlie Roots and Chris Staargaard. Geological Association of Canada.

Bridge, Josephine and June C. West. (no date). *The University of British Columbia Botanical Garden.* Vancouver.

Forster, Roy. 1993. *VanDusen Botanical Garden Guidebook.* VanDusen Botanical Garden, Vancouver.

Forster, Roy. 1985. *Observations on Design, Plant Collections and Construction.* VanDusen Botanical Garden, Vancouver.

Livingston, William. 1956. *From a Water Filled Quarry to a Beautiful and Growing Arboretum.* (publication details unavailable, copy on file at VanDusen Botanical Garden).

Lyons, C.P. and Bill Merrilees. 1995. *Trees, Flowers & Shrubs to Know in B.C.* Lone Pine, Vancouver.

Steele, Mike. 1993. *Stanley Park.* Heritage House Publishing Company, Surrey, BC.

Straley, Gerald. 1992. *Trees of Vancouver.* University of British Columbia Press, Vancouver.

Stubbs, Betty. 1985. *From Golf Course to Garden: A History of VanDusen Botanical Display Gardens.* Vancouver Botanical Gardens, Vancouver.

Vancouver Natural History Society. 1995. *The Birds of Burrard Inlet.* Vancouver Natural History Society, Vancouver.

Vancouver Natural History Society. 1993. *A Bird Watching Guide to the Vancouver Area, British Columbia.* Cavendish Books, North Vancouver.

Vancouver Natural History Society. 1988. *Nature West Coast.* (2nd ed.). Sono Nis Press, Victoria.

Vancouver Natural History Society. 1988. *The Natural History of Stanley Park.* Vancouver Natural History Society, Vancouver.